The A̶ of Investing

Second Edition

Dean A. Junkans

ANATOMY: *The art of separating or dividing something into parts for detailed examination.*

INVESTING: *The act of committing (money) in order to earn a financial return.*

Strategic Book Publishing and Rights Co.

Strategic Book Publishing and Rights Co.
12620 FM 1960, Suite A4-507
Houston, TX 77065
www.sbpra.com

ISBN: 978-1-61897-388-7

Typography and page composition by J. K. Eckert & Company

Endorsements

"This book is easily one of the best and most readable investment primers I've come across during my 45 years in the business. It's a great way to learn about basic investment concepts and how they can be applied to almost anyone's situation."

—William B. Frels, CFA, Chairman and CEO,
Mairs and Power

"If only I had access to your book when I got my first job, I know I could have done much better with my investments. This book should be read by anyone who wants an easy to understand, interesting and practical guide to investing.
I am going to give a copy to my daughter!"

—Kjell R. Knudsen, Ph.D., Dean, Labovitz School of
Business and Economics, University of Minnesota Duluth

"The Anatomy of Investing is a full-bodied tour of the ins and outs of planning for one's financial future and avoiding the vast number of pitfalls that face individual investors every day. Uncluttered by finance-speak and thoughtfully organized, Dean brings to his subject a wealth of experience and practical advice. From beginning to end, it's clear that he cares deeply about both his subject and the everyday investors he's trying to help."

—Tony Carideo, CFA, President, The Carideo Group, Inc.

"Dean Junkans has been a key thought leader for us on investment strategy and asset allocation for many years. Now everyone can benefit from his well thought out views on investing. The Anatomy of Investing is a terrific resource for anyone interested in learning more about the foundation of successful investing. Ignore the promises made by those who advocate the home run trades to riches approach. This book will equip the reader with the understanding and right tools to build a sound and diversified investment decision making approach which has been the hallmark of the industry's best money managers."

—Jay Welker, Executive Vice President and Head of the
Wealth Management Group at Wells Fargo

Contents

Foreword

By Joel Larson, MD

The human body is a sophisticated, highly integrated composition of unique organ systems. These organ systems work together reacting to changing conditions in order to optimize the body's health, well-being and performance. We all have a basic understanding of these individual organ systems and the role they play in our body's homeostasis. The author has used this basic knowledge of human anatomy and physiology as an analogy to the unique features (organ systems) of a healthy financial portfolio. By doing so the author has created a process of sharing and teaching financial planning that is both simple and entertaining. I found myself curious about which organ system would represent which part of a financial portfolio and how well the analogy would work as a teaching tool. I welcomed with anticipation the portfolio priorities comparing them with the importance of an organ system always realizing that all organ systems were necessary for an optimally functioning body.

By using this analogy to teach financial planning the author has simplified and refocused the features of a financial plan in such a way that readers will better understand these financial tools and their place in a financial portfolio.

Start reading and you will enjoy the anatomy lesson as you learn about your investment portfolio.

Have fun! This, too, is an important feature of staying healthy and becoming wealthy.

Acknowledgments

Thank you to my family who believed that I could somehow find the time to revise and update The Anatomy of Investing. Thank you, Tammie, Erin and Daniel.

Thanks to all my colleagues at Wells Fargo who have been continually supportive of my writing over the past several years.

Thanks to the team at Strategic Book Publishing who work together to take the written word and create a book and provide high touch support to the author through the whole process.

This book would not have been possible without the support of my executive assistant, Sally Bjerke, and the help and encouragement from Sarah Douglass in our marketing department. They were really the glue that kept this project together. I owe both a huge thank you!

Introduction

I grew up on a dairy farm in Wisconsin and, at a relatively early age, was more interested in investing than I was in tractors, combines, or cows. Nearly every spare dollar I earned was invested in either mutual funds or ham radio equipment, my other passion at the time.

One of the greatest benefits of growing up on a farm is gaining an appreciation for hard work. A second benefit is learning how to focus on the long term. This is especially important when crop and milk prices or the weather do not cooperate in the short run. And third, you get a close view (sometimes too close) of how simple, yet complex, the world and everything in it can be.

Thirty years after leaving farm life, having for the most part converted to being a certified (hopefully not certifiable) city person, I have retained many of those same views of the world. As a result, I thought I would take a subject that has become a career and a passion for me—investing—and break it down in a simple approach using human anatomy as a guide.

Out of the blue it occurred to me that there are many parallels between human anatomy and a successful investment process for the individual investor. In the human body, a number of key organs and body parts must work together to sustain life. An individual investment portfolio, the various parts of it, and the individuals managing it, must also work together to have a sustainable and successful experience.

My intent in this book is to outline a basic approach to investing that nearly any investor can understand and implement, either on their own or with the help and guidance of an advisor. If you are looking for a book that goes in depth into new breathtaking investment approaches, this will not be the book to purchase. If you are looking for a quick and easy way to make money in the market, this book will be of little use to you. If, however, you are willing to work hard and focus on the long term or, if you grew up on a farm or always wished to, please read on.

In this book I will match ten basic parts of our human anatomy to the principles of a successful investment experience. This book will explore each of these principles in a separate chapter. Each chapter provides an explanation of these principles in layman's terms rather than typical investment jargon and will include some examples of how real investors or their advisors can implement them.

Because I do not believe that you can separate an individual investment plan from the individual, I have also touched on some financial planning concepts that would normally be covered in a separate book. I make no apologies for not following the prescribed tradition of separating investing from personal finance, as I have never understood how that tradition makes sense.

In order to help you craft your own game plan, I have organized each chapter with a summary called Healthy Investment Tips. These tips highlight and summarize the important points for you to consider as you invest your money. My intent is to address topics that can help you wherever you are in your investment journey, and regardless of whether you are doing it on your own or with the help of a professional advisor.

I hope you find that this book offers many useful investment ideas and maybe you will learn a little about anatomy along the way!

Note to the Reader

The publisher and author have presented the information and ideas in this book on a best-efforts basis, but do not warranty the accuracy or completeness of the content or strategies discussed. The advice, ideas, and strategies contained herein may not be suitable for your particular situation. You should consult with a professional, as appropriate. Neither the publisher nor the author shall be liable for any loss or damages of any kind resulting from action taken or not taken from this publication.

1

Learning to Walk: The Difference Between Saving and Investing

Walking: The act of moving your body with your legs and feet

Some people never get beyond the crawling stage. They crawl from one thing to the next without a thought about where to crawl next. This approach of carefree living and spontaneity can be very appealing. It may even be okay for you, as long as you are only responsible for yourself and nothing in your life goes wrong, and as long as you do not care if you have any money on which to fund your retirement. If you *are* concerned about this, however, stop crawling and learn to walk.

When it comes to investing, going from saving to investing is like going from crawling to walking. Sometimes saving and investing are used synonymously, yet like crawling and walking, they are very different. The notion of saving is best described as the act of setting aside and accumulating money for a specific purpose. The specific purpose could be buying a car, taking a vacation, purchasing furniture, accumulating an emergency fund, etc. In other words, savings is money that you are setting aside now, but will likely spend in the future.

Investing, on the other hand, is money that you will live on in the future. Think of it as building a foundation that will provide you with spendable income down the road. Investing allows you to build a portfolio that will generate income and returns that will someday allow you to buy things that you used to save for from your regular income. I found one definition of walking that called it "the act of taking steps." Investing is also a process of taking steps. I will discuss these steps in Chapter 12.

It is important to understand that you can save and you can invest regardless of your income level. I often hear people say that they don't make enough money to save, much less invest. I do believe there is some income level at which you need all your income for food, shelter, and clothing. For some, however, perhaps this list of basic necessities becomes food, shelter, clothing, and more clothing, the latest electronic gadgets, luxury cars, and fancy vacations. In other words, if you really are tapped out but are serious about saving and investing, you may need to ask yourself if you are willing to give up some of these things to get beyond the crawling stage.

LIVING BELOW YOUR MEANS VERSUS LIVING WITHIN YOUR MEANS

This is a critical issue if you want to create some financial margin in your life. What am I talking about here? You have likely heard the phrase, "too many needs chasing too few dollars." Many people can probably relate to that, and they almost automatically know what it means. I would maintain that, in many cases, the problem is simply too many needs. These are needs that started as wants and, over time, became needs. These needs then require more dollars to fulfill.

I am sure you have read some articles on the importance of living within your means. In my opinion, the notion of living within your means misses the mark. Living *below* your means is a better way to save, invest, grow your wealth, and just plain live. Okay, so what's the difference?

Living within your means implies spending all your income, but no more than your income. This is certainly preferable to spending more than you make. However, unless you inherited a large amount of money or you plan to cash out of a business in the not too distant future, this is not a recipe to accumulate wealth. Living below your means implies not spending everything you make. In other words, earmarking a portion of your income to either saving or investing. In addition to saving and investing, living below your means gives you financial margin in your life.

Having financial margin in your life allows you to deal with unexpected expenses or take advantage of unexpected opportunities. These expenses or opportunities could take the form of a spontaneous vacation, helping a child pay for a wedding, donating funds to a charitable need that arises, and so on. Having this margin in your life puts less stress on your overall financial plan and can help with your overall peace of mind.

My recommendation is to draw very strict boundaries between accounts you use for savings and those you use for investments. I would further recommend that you have the following accounts set up:

1. **Emergency savings account:** This is a sum of money that is not earmarked for anything in particular. It is for an emergency. That emergency could be the loss of a job, an unexpected house or car repair, etc.

   There is a tremendous amount of advice out there on how big this account should be. Most of the advice is centered on having enough in this account to handle all of your basic living expenses for some period of time, typically ranging from three to six months. If you are living paycheck to paycheck, don't think you can't save for this account. My advice is to do *something;* don't become discouraged and do nothing.

   My personal view is that with more and more employers paying their employees a salary and an annual bonus, the annual bonus could be a great way to jumpstart an emergency savings account. Rather than look at the bonus as just more discretionary income, stash some of it in this savings account.

   If you do not get any type of bonuses throughout the year, start with a smaller goal and celebrate the success along the way. For many investors, it is unrealistic to be able to stash away six months' worth of living expenses. Instead, start with the goal of stashing away two paychecks' worth of living expenses and build from there. If you do not receive an annual bonus, ask your employer's payroll department to deduct $50 to

$100 from every check to automatically go into a savings account and get your fund started that way.

2. **Savings accounts for specific purchases:** This could be for any type of expense, ranging from a vacation to a car to a house project. Personally, I think it is useful to have a separate account for each major item, such as savings for a house or a car, so you can track the progress of saving for each one. I know this sounds old-fashioned with the advent of home equity loans, multiple credit cards, second and third mortgages, and so on, but, if you want to actually enjoy these purchases rather than stress out about how you are going to pay for them, sometimes old-fashioned is not so bad.

3. **Investment accounts:** These are for long-term investing. I suggest you have at least two types of investment accounts: your tax-qualified accounts—such as your individual retirement account (IRA), 401(k), 403(b), etc.—and your taxable accounts. Investing money in taxable accounts will provide you with assets and a stream of income should you want to retire before your normal retirement age. (Note that if you have not invested any money in a taxable account in addition to your tax-qualified accounts, it is probably a pipe dream that you will be able to retire early.)

My advice on your retirement investment accounts is to never borrow from them, even if your tax-qualified plan may allow you to do so easily. This will potentially slow down the amount of assets you accumulate in your retirement plan, and you will receive no tax benefit from the interest you pay yourself as you pay back the account.

If you change employers, roll your tax-qualified plan into either the new employer's plan or an IRA, and enroll in new contributions as soon as possible. Frequently, investors "cash in" or take a distribution from their old plan, which can derail their long-term investment plans as well as result in sizeable tax and penalty hits.

Additionally, never, *ever* take money out of your investment accounts for any reason before you retire. If you develop the bad habit of doing so, it will be hard to break and it will likely throw you off track toward accumulating a sufficient nest egg for the future.

Healthy Investment Tips

1. Separate your savings from your investments.
2. Separate your savings into accounts for specific purchases versus emergency needs.
3. Hold your investment accounts sacred. Do not borrow from them, and never, ever take money out of them for any reason prior to retirement.
4. Live below your means to create financial margin in your life.

2

Self-Discovery: The Development of Investment Goals

Discovery: The act of searching for or learning something previously unknown to you

Self-discovery is an important aspect of everyday life. It seems as if we are continually learning about ourselves and the world in which we live. Just as self-discovery is a continual process, so, too, is the development of investment goals for the individual investor. Not enough is written about this topic, yet it is a critical issue for individual investors to consider before they get started on their investment journey and at rest stops along the way. The first thing you need to figure out is your goals.

HOW TO DETERMINE YOUR GOALS

Investment advisors often sit down with an investor and try to determine the investor's goals by identifying his or her level of risk tolerance—or the amount of risk an investor is prepared to take to achieve a certain level of return. The practice of determining risk tolerance is based on modern portfolio theory and assumes that the investor has one, and only one, level of risk tolerance. The higher the return you seek, the higher the potential risk to your investments from market fluctuations. Typically, the longer the time horizon, the more risk you can afford to take. However, in reviewing your situation, you may realize that you do not have just one investment goal or level of risk tolerance; you may have many relating to both your short- and long-term needs and goals.

Your portfolio should be designed to satisfy an entire life cycle of needs. The basic needs of food, clothing, and shelter come first. Beyond that, you may want to consider your lifestyle, education, retirement, philanthropic, and legacy goals. You should set aside specific money for each goal and invest each pool of money based upon your unique risk, return, liquidity, cash flow, and tax requirements for that goal. So when someone asks what your risk tolerance is, the answer should be, "That depends on which pool of assets you are asking about."

Figure 1 highlights the major requirements or needs that you likely expect your portfolio to support. Typically, investors have four broad categories of needs:

Figure 1 Your Starting Point: What is the Money For?

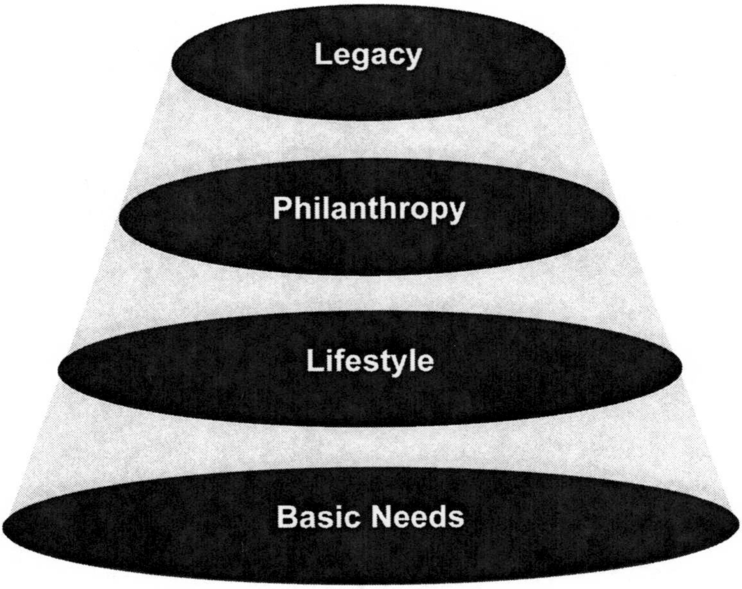

Source: © 2006 Wells Fargo Bank, N.A. All rights reserved. Used with permission from Wells Fargo Bank, N. A.

1. **Basic:** Meeting your food, shelter, and immediate lifestyle necessities
2. **Lifestyle:** Maintaining a satisfactory or specific lifestyle throughout your life
3. **Philanthropy:** Supporting causes or charities that you are passionate about
4. **Legacy:** Making significant bequests during or after your lifetime

Within these categories, there are five sets of beneficiaries that you may need to consider:

1. Yourself
2. Spouse/partner
3. Children/heirs
4. Society
5. Government

There are five parameters that will need to be optimized in your portfolio for a successful experience:

1. **Return:** Your need for a particular level of return
2. **Risk:** The potential fluctuations in the value of your investments, which could result in losses
3. **Liquidity:** The degree to which you need your portfolio assets to be easily convertible to cash
4. **Cash flow:** Your need for reliable cash flow from your portfolio
5. **Tax efficiency:** Your need to reduce the impact of taxes on your after-tax portfolio returns prior to retirement; only applicable to your taxable accounts

Once you have determined your needs, goals, beneficiaries, and parameters, then it is time to determine how you can set up portfolios to meet these needs. The process is best started by writing down your thoughts in each of these areas and then quantifying the investment returns required to successfully accomplish them.

Lastly, the process of self-discovery is never-ending. Whether you are talking about your life, in general, or your investment goals, you are always learning more and fine-tuning as a result. Keep that in mind as you regularly revisit your investment goals. Remember that they may change as your life changes.

MENTAL ACCOUNTING AND DECISION AVOIDANCE

The last topic I want to address in this chapter is the value of mental accounting and the danger of what I call "decision avoidance." During periods of market stress or lack of confidence, it is easy to get into a funk where you don't even want to think about your goals or your long-term investment plan. The result of this can be avoiding making important long-term portfolio decisions that can have detrimental long-term effects on your portfolio. A way to help deal with that is going through the process I described above, but adding another layer to help mentally account for your portfolio in three distinct buckets.

The three buckets of portfolio mental accounting are described below:

1. **The Liquidity Bucket:** This is essentially the cash you need to satisfy cash flow and liquidity requirements that are known over the next several months. In my opinion, if you can have at least twelve months covered, that should give you some degree of financial margin in your life. Additionally, you may want to hold extra cash or liquidity that provides you with additional peace of mind and that will allow you to stick with your long-term investment plan when you really do not want to. This number will vary greatly by investor—some investors will not need much extra liquidity and others will need much more. There is no magic formula that will tell you how much to have in this portion of the bucket; it is something you will need to think about and discuss with your advisor.

2. **The Growth and Income Bucket:** This part of the portfolio generates growth of principal over time and provides the major portion of investors' income needs. In this bucket, it also important to think about how investments are positioned for income and how they can also grow the income over time, rather than just be stagnant or subject to changing market interest rates. While this bucket will include different types of bonds and fixed-income investments, having some exposure to income-producing real estate and equity dividends with growth potential will help address this issue. This part of the portfolio needs to be calibrated to the investor's

long-term financial goals; therefore, the investor should be careful not to let his or her emotions during difficult market environments derail this core bucket.

3. **The Skeptics Bucket:** If the worst fears of an investor come true in regard to the market, this is the portion of the portfolio that can help smooth the ride. Investors may want to consider hedging strategies and alternative investments for this part of the portfolio. Many of these strategies will help reduce downside risk in the portfolio and may do relatively well in certain difficult market conditions. Investors really need to do their due diligence to make sure they understand this part of the portfolio and how it can help the whole portfolio. Ideally, investors should work with an advisor who can help explain and provide education on these types of investments.

If an investor has the right mix of his or her portfolio in each of these three buckets and mentally thinks about his or her portfolio in this context, it may be helpful in not letting emotions derail long-term investment plans.

Healthy Investment Tips

1. Identify your investment goals.
2. Document these goals, the purpose of the goals, and who benefits from them.
3. Start thinking about what type of portfolios best meets these goals.
4. Mental accounting can be a useful way to think about your portfolio and avoid reacting emotionally or not making decisions at all regarding your long-term investment plan.

3

The Spine: The Backbone of Your Portfolio

Spine: A flexible, rod-like structure that forms the supporting axis of the body

The spine is also referred to as the backbone. A very simple definition of backbone is "the main support" structure, or the main sustaining piece of the body. In terms of investing, the backbone of your investment portfolio should be centered on asset allocation and the distribution of your personal assets into different asset classes.

In this section, I will explore the basic concepts necessary to start investing—the backbone of your investment journey. The first area I will cover is the type of investments to consider. There are several types of investments; in the investment world, they are generally called "asset classes." These include stocks, bonds, real estate, commodities, cash, and alternatives or complementary strategies. Each of these asset classes has a distinct purpose within your portfolio and, combined together in the right mix, they represent the backbone of your portfolio.

The returns and the risks associated with each of these asset classes vary considerably. Figure 2 shows how the returns of these asset classes can vary from year to year.

Figure 2 Returns by Asset Class

Asset Class	June-99	June-00	June-01	June-02	June-03	June-04	June-05	June-06	June-07	June-08	June-09	June-10	June-11
S&P 500	22.76	7.25	-14.83	-17.99	0.25	19.11	6.32	8.63	20.59	-13.12	-26.21	14.43	30.69
Large Cap	21.92	9.25	-14.96	-17.88	0.95	19.48	7.92	9.08	20.43	-12.36	-26.69	15.23	31.93
Mid Cap	11.31	12.64	0.96	-9.23	2.63	29.39	17.12	13.66	20.83	-11.19	-30.36	25.13	38.47
Small Cap	1.5	14.32	0.57	-8.6	-1.64	33.36	9.45	14.58	16.43	-16.19	-25.01	21.48	37.41
Intermediate Government	4.43	4.48	10.42	8.58	8.62	0.48	4.14	0.07	5.43	9.17	6.42	5.68	2.65
Intermediate BAA Corp	3.45	3.26	10.39	4.61	15.66	1.47	5.76	-0.87	6.93	2.98	5.27	16.98	7.59
Aggregate Bond	3.15	4.57	11.23	8.63	10.4	0.32	6.8	-0.81	6.12	7.12	6.05	9.5	3.9
1-3 Month T-Bill	4.78	5.38	5.7	2.45	1.42	0.89	2.04	3.98	5.11	3.31	0.77	0.12	0.14
REIT	-8.98	3.03	24.43	16.21	4	27.06	32.66	19.06	12.57	-13.64	-43.29	53.9	34.09
EAFE	7.92	17.44	23.51	-9.22	-6.06	32.85	14.13	27.07	27.54	-10.15	30.96	6.38	30.93
Commodity	10.42	33.84	2.19	0.17	17.91	25.61	8.56	18.09	2.94	41.56	-47.08	2.75	25.91
Emerging Market	28.71	9.43	-25.89	1.31	6.96	33.51	34.89	35.91	45.45	4.89	-27.82	23.48	28.17

Data Source: MPI Stylus, June 30, 2011

Markov Processes International, LLC

As you can see, in some asset classes, returns vary considerably from year to year. In other asset classes, returns may not appear to be substantially different. But, over a long period of time, the return differences can be substantial. This is what is called the "power of time." What happens is that the returns earned in one year are compounded, meaning that you start earning returns on returns. Over time, this can really be significant.

Figure 3 shows how compounding works over time. The example illustrates how much impact just a 1 percent difference in return can make over various periods of time. Additionally, the example highlights how much it matters when you start your investment journey.

As you can see from Figure 3, a 1 percent difference in return over a forty-year time period on a starting portfolio of $25,000 can make a difference of as much as $250,000! A quarter of a million dollars is a pretty tangible example of the power of time and the related power of compounding returns.

BASIC ASSET CLASSES DEFINED

Stocks

If you own a stock, you basically own a piece of a company that is documented by your "stock holding." Stocks are often referred to as equities because a stockholder is essentially an equity owner in that particular company.

When investors think about stock ownership, they typically think of traded or public stock. However, in many cases, investors can invest in private stock as well. Private stock is often referred to as "private equity." The primary difference in private stock versus publicly traded stock is its illiquidity. Investors in private stock are typically required to hold the stock for several years before they are able to sell it or realize any returns. Public stock, in contrast, is traded on public stock exchanges—such as the New York Stock Exchange (NYSE)—where an investor can get instant pricing and buy and sell the stock on a daily basis.

Generally, stocks provide investors with returns from four potential sources. One source of return on a stock is its appreciation potential. This appreciation potential is typically the result of the company performing well, as measured by earnings growth or other metrics. The earnings growth of a

Figure 3   The Power of Time

Annual Return	Value After 10 Years	Value After 20 Years	Value After 30 Years	Value After 40 Years
5%	$40,722	$66,332	$108,049	$176,000
6%	$44,771	$80,179	$143,587	$257,143
7%	$49,179	$96,742	$190,306	$374,361
8%	$53,973	$116,524	$251,566	$543,113
9%	$59,184	$140,110	$331,692	$785,235
10%	$64,843	$168,187	$436,235	$1,131,481

Data Source: Author's Analysis, using a starting portfolio of $25,000 company can be divided between growth that is due to general levels of inflation in the economy and the rate of growth above that of the rate of inflation, which is also referred to as real growth.

In an environment where the overall stock market is trending higher, the stock could appreciate simply because the price level of most stocks is being repriced at higher levels, or higher valuations. This source of return is often referred to as "P/E expansion" in reference to a typical way in which stocks are valued in the market—price relative to earnings.

Another important source of returns comes from dividends, or the return of a portion of the earnings to the owners. The reinvestment of dividends over time can also have a significant impact on overall stock returns, and I will explore that in more detail in Chapter 10.

Figure 4 shows the potential sources of return from stocks and how each has contributed to stock returns historically over time.

Figure 4   Components of Returns from Stocks

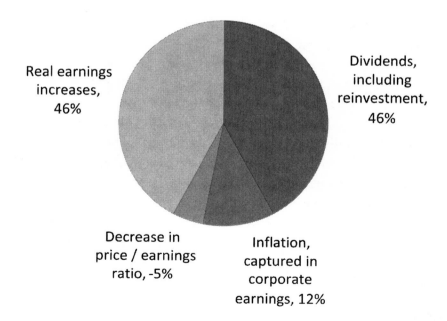

Data Source: Bloomberg Finance, L.P., December 2010

From 1987 to 2010, Standard and Poor's (S&P) 500 generated annualized returns of 9.9 percent. The above pie chart shows the components of those returns. You can see that, historically, dividends and the reinvestment of dividends were tied with real earnings growth for the largest source of return.

While this data can be a helpful guide, it is important to note that the contributions of these sources of return can vary substantially based on current market conditions—most notably, current levels of valuation and the point in the economic cycle—and on the type of stocks you purchase. The second decade of 2000 started in an environment where dividend payouts as a percentage of earnings were low. In this kind of environment, where companies are reinvesting more of their earnings in the company than they are paying out to shareholders in the form of dividends, you could expect the source of return from earnings growth to be high. However, the low payout of dividends can set the stage from which dividends can increase if companies decide to return more of their earnings to shareholders.

Another perspective on stock returns can be found in Appendix VII. I have included a series of charts titled "Asset Class Returns by Holding Period" that are a fifty-year look at stock price returns over various time periods. For example, in any fifteen-year or more period of time, U.S. large cap stocks have always provided investors with positive returns. (This is data through May 2011.) In contrast, ten-year and under rolling time periods have given investors the potential of a negative return.

The range of possible outcomes for ten-year annualized returns varies from a negative 3.43 percent to a positive 21.43 percent. If you drop down to three-year holding periods, the range of outcomes varies from negative 16.09 percent to positive 33.30 percent. A twenty-year timeframe gives you an annual return range of 6.41 percent to 18.26 percent. The moral of the story here is that the longer the timeframe, the better the potential result for stock investors.

Bonds

If you own a bond, you are basically a lender to a company or to the government (if you own U.S. Treasury bonds). In return for lending this money, you will generally get a fixed rate of interest over the length of time during which the bond is held. The money is paid out in the form of a coupon. Alternatively, many companies issue what are called "floating rate" bonds, where the rate of interest you receive is adjusted periodically based on the prevailing levels of interest rates in the market.

Typically, the interest rate you receive is based on the credit quality or credit worthiness of the company. Quite simply, this refers to the probability of you—the investor—getting your money back when the bond matures (when it comes due). Generally, the lower the quality of the bond, the higher the interest rate you can expect to receive. This higher interest rate, in theory, compensates the investor for taking a higher degree of risk. The higher the credit quality (the lower the risk), the lower your interest rate will be.

The main source of returns from bonds is the income you receive. Many investors who held bond funds in the 1980s and 1990s believe that bonds can produce returns above the income level of a specific bond. This was true for a while as the general level of interest rates plummeted in the '80s and '90s, providing a boost to bond returns in the form of capital appreciation. At lower levels of interest rates, it is unlikely that bond holders will experience much appreciation, and the chances of losing principal to higher interest rates becomes a greater risk. If bonds are sold prior to maturity, you may receive more or less than your original investment, based on the prevailing level of interest rates and the amount of time the bond has until it matures.

Many investors believe that rising interest rates are good for their bond investments. Refer to the survey of investors and their view on interest rates and how they impact bond prices (Figure 5).

The reverse is generally true. The market is willing to pay less for bonds that pay out interest below the current levels of rates set by the market. Figure 6 demonstrates how the movement of interest rates influences the price of bonds at different maturities. The longer the maturity, the greater the sensitivity to interest rate movements. A 2 percent increase in interest rates results in a 3.77 percent loss of principal on a two-year maturity bond. The same 2 percent rate increase results in a 16.03 percent loss of principal on a ten-year maturity bond.

Figure 5 Percentage of Investors Who Do Not Understand How Interest Rate Changes Impact Their Portfolio

> $3 Million	69%
$1 - $3 Million	71%
Use An Advisor	76%
Self-Directed	58%

As you can see from Fig. 6, the level of interest rates also affects how much interest rate movements impact the price of bonds. For example, at a coupon of 1 percent lower on the ten-year bond, the duration is two-thirds of a year longer, meaning that a rise in interest rates in a lower interest rate environment will have an even bigger impact on price, all other things being equal.

Bonds can be purchased in a variety of ways. If you have a large enough portfolio—typically $250,000 or more dedicated to bonds—you can buy individual issues. You usually need to buy these through a broker, who make a spread that is effectively their commission. This spread reduces the yield, or effective interest rate, you will receive on the bond. If you buy bonds this way, it is important to understand the current level of interest rates in the market for the type and maturity of bond you are purchasing to ensure that you are getting an attractive yield. If you do not have access to that information, another alternative is to ask two or more brokers to provide you with current pricing on the same bond.

Figure 6 Bond Return Sensitivity to Interest Rate Movement

Years to Maturity	2 Years	5 Years	10 Years	30 Years
Current Yield (6/29/11)	.38%	1.55%	3.00%	4.23%
+ 50 bps	.88%	2.05%	3.50%	4.73%
Projected Price Impact	-0.96%	-2.36%	-4.31%	-8.23%
+ 100 bps	1.38%	2.55%	4.00%	5.23%
Projected Price Impact	-1.91%	-4.66%	-8.41%	-15.51%
+ 200 bps	2.38%	3.55%	5.00%	6.23%
Projected Price Impact	-3.77%	-9.08%	-16.03%	-27.07%

Price impact (projected) based on modified duration (x) interest rate change over a 12 month time horizon.

Data Source: Bloomberg Finance, L.P and Author Analysis, June 2011

Investors with less than $250,000 should, in most cases, buy bonds through mutual funds, exchange-traded funds (ETFs), or closed-end funds (CEFs). Be careful when buying a bond fund that you understand the level of ongoing expenses as well as any upfront or back-end charges. When interest rates are relatively low, expenses can substantially reduce your return.

Real Estate

This is the ownership of real or tangible property. Real estate investing can take many forms. In its most common form, it could mean your home. In spite of a general long-term appreciation of home prices over time, I do not often think of your personal residence as a real estate investment. You cannot realize the gains from appreciation unless you sell your home, and you may need the proceeds to be put toward another home. Real estate, as an investment, is generally described as property that produces some appreciation potential over time, but also a steady and regular flow of income.

Real estate investments include apartment or office buildings, shopping or retail properties, storage facilities, and commercial properties. Investors can access these investments through five primary vehicles:

1. Public real estate investment trusts (REITs)
2. Private REITs
3. Real estate private placements
4. Real estate mutual funds
5. Real estate ETFs

Much like the stock market, investors in real estate should consider not only diversifying by the sector, or category, of real estate, they should also consider both domestic and international real estate opportunities.

Commodities

Investing in commodities is often referred to as "investing in hard assets." This asset class encompasses precious metals such as gold and silver; industrial metals such as copper and zinc; agricultural commodities such as corn and cattle; and energy commodities such as oil and natural gas.

Investing in commodities used to be quite difficult for private investors. Historically, the primary way to invest in commodities was to simply take physical delivery of the commodity. The act of taking physical
delivery presented numerous problems for the investor, not the least of
which was storage costs and the need to have insurance against potential
loss or theft.

Commodity investing now is much easier for investors as a range of
investment vehicles—ETFs, mutual funds, CEFs, private placements, and
structured notes—are being used to provide access to this asset class. The
main source of return from commodities is the potential appreciation in the
price of the commodity you own. Commodities generally provide no direct
income or dividend to the investor. This is an important consideration for
investors needing a high level of income from their investments. From a
portfolio perspective, commodities can be used to provide a partial hedge
against inflation and as a diversifier to both stocks and bonds.

As the investment landscape has become global, and the income levels
of people from around the world has increased, so, too, has their consumption of commodities. At the end of 2010*, China alone accounted for more
than 41 percent of refined copper; 42 percent of semi-refined nickel; 45
percent of refined tin; 46 percent of zinc slab; 48 percent of refined lead
consumption; 42 percent of cotton consumption; 16 percent of wheat consumption; 20 percent of corn; 25 percent of soybeans; 31 percent of rice;
48 percent of coal consumption; and more than 10 percent of oil demand.
As emerging economies around the world, such as China and India, continue to emerge and grow, the demand for commodities will likely continue
to increase, creating a potentially interesting opportunity for investors in
this asset class.[1]

Figure 7 illustrates how demographics will provide an important under-
pinning to long-term commodity demand. As you can see, the age distribution in emerging market economies is skewed heavily toward youth, which
will provide additional demand pressures on commodity resources in the
future.

---

[1] Sources: Bloomberg, U.S. Department of Agriculture, Bloomberg, British Petroleum
Statistical Review, Bloomberg, World Bureau of Metal Statistics

Figure 7   Global Age Distribution

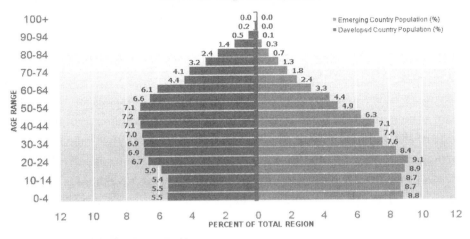

Global Age Distribution
as % of Regional Population

Alternatives

It is difficult to categorize alternatives as an asset class because there are potentially several different types of assets that can be included here. Investments often considered as alternatives (complementary strategies) include hedge funds, private equity, venture capital, and structured products.

The primary commonality in the alternative investment space is the non-correlation, or low-correlation, benefits they exhibit relative to traditional investments, such as common stocks. In other words, they tend to move in a different cycle. If the stock market is declining, some alternative investments may be appreciating, and vice versa. Alternative investments often come with higher fees (including performance-based fees) as well as a higher degree of illiquidity than traditional investments. Investment success in alternatives is often due to manager skill and the related ability of the manager to exploit opportunities in the market.

Beware of products you do not or cannot understand. There is a lot of creativity in the financial services industry around product creation. Make sure you understand the product and, most importantly, what, if anything, it will accomplish in the context of your overall portfolio. The potential benefit of alternatives is to help smooth volatility in the context of the investor's entire portfolio.

Investors in alternatives need to have a long investment time horizon. They also need an understanding of the illiquid nature of this asset class—it may be difficult or impossible to access your money for a specified period of possibly several years in some cases—and the strategies and risks taken (including leverage and concentrated bets) to achieve the results.

Cash

There is some debate among investment professionals on whether cash is its own distinct asset class. It seems to me that the answer to this debate does not matter very much. Cash is clearly an option for individuals. "How much cash do you need for liquidity purposes or for peace of mind?" and "What are your other options?" are the appropriate questions to ask.

I have found that many investors have a specific dollar amount in mind that they want to hold, regardless of actual liquidity needs. This varies greatly by investor, and there is no magic formula to arrive at the number. I know some investors who have the attitude that if everything else in their portfolio is going down, they want to have X amount of dollars safe and sound. For some investors, that number might be $100,000; for others, that might be $1 million or more.

The number is the level of liquidity, or cash level, individual investors should maintain to handle the next several months of cash flow needs as well as any additional cushion that will help them sleep well at night during periods of market volatility. If investors do not have enough liquidity in their portfolios, they will want and sometimes even need to act to raise liquidity when prices are often disadvantageous to do so. Or they may be tempted to simply abandon long-term plans, many times after the damage has already been done.

There is no black box, no asset allocation model, and no manual to read that will tell exactly how much cash or liquidity an investor needs to have. This is a very personal decision, based on an individual's emotional wiring, tolerance for risk, cash needs, and anticipated or potential cash needs. Your investment professional can help you talk through this and arrive at the number. Ultimately, it is your decision.

As you can see from Figure 8, investors often have a specific dollar amount in mind when they think about their cash target. In only a little more than one-third of the time do they have a specific percentage of the portfolio in mind as a cash target.

Figure 8   How Do You Think About Your Cash Target?

Specific Dollar Amount in Mind	28%
Specific Percent of Portfolio in Mind	35%
No Specific Target in Mind	37%

Holding cash in the form of currency in your wallet, in your dresser drawers, or in your safe may provide some psychological benefit, but beyond that, it makes little sense. Investors can hold cash more productively in interest-bearing accounts that provide daily liquidity (or access to the money), but pay the investor some interest.

Money market accounts or funds and bank savings accounts are the most common forms of interest-bearing accounts used by investors. Be wary of investments touted as enhanced money market accounts. They may pay a higher rate of interest, but they may also have higher risk of principal loss.

Healthy Investment Tips

1. The backbone of your portfolio is the asset classes that make up your portfolio.
2. Before you establish your asset allocation (or distribution of assets into the various asset classes), you should have a good understanding of the purpose of each asset class in your portfolio.
3. Once you have a good understanding of each asset class, you can start thinking about what type of investment vehicles are best suited for you as you get exposure to the different assets in your portfolio.
4. Before you do anything, go through the discovery process of the level of cash/liquidity you need and the additional amount you need to sleep well at night. I refer to this as your "number."

4

The Brain: Right Brain and Left Brain Roles in Investing

Brain: *The primary center for the regulation and control of bodily activities; receives and interprets sensory impulses, and transmits information to the muscles and body organs*

Your investing journey must start with your brain. It seems logical enough, but many investors don't realize this. Instead, they tend to start with their arms and legs (the significance of arms and legs is discussed in Chapter 12) because they just want to do *something.* This action can give investors a sense of control, and for some activities in life, this approach can make total sense. For successful investing, however, it does not. Why? Because you need a plan.

Investors often ask me what I like in the market. They may have some cash to invest, and so they ask me what stocks I prefer or what mutual funds are attractive. Or they read about ideas in the financial media and they act on that information. The problem with this approach is that it is analogous to jumping in a car with a vague idea of a destination, but no map. You will end up burning a lot of gas, and you might not ever get to the destination you hoped for. These people are using the right side of their brains—the random, intuitive, and subjective part—and that's probably not the best place to start.

You do not have to be a genius to be a successful investor. A study completed by staff at Ohio State University found that people with a high IQ were no wealthier than people with average intelligence. A colleague of mine likes to say, "You need to be smart about the market, not smarter than the market." I have yet to see someone who is smarter than the market. To be a successful investor, you need three things: a game plan, discipline, and patience. Let's start first with the game plan.

LEFT BRAIN: THE INVESTMENT PLAN

The left brain is said to be the logical, sequential, rationale, analytical, and objective part of the brain. That sounds like music to my ears, or better said, it sounds like a plan! Many individual investors do not develop an investment plan. If they have a plan, they do not put it in writing or use it as a roadmap for their investing. As a result, their portfolios often end up being a collection of ideas that were pitched to them, that they read about, or that were recommended to them. It will be pure luck if a portfolio put together with this approach successfully meets your goals.

A more objective (another left brain reference) approach is to create an investment policy statement (IPS). The purpose of the IPS is to spell out your investment goals, your objectives, and specific guidelines you want to address in the management of your investment portfolio. At a minimum, I believe that an IPS should include the following five elements:

1. Standards for the management of the assets held in your portfolio. Specifically, you may want to address:

   a. Asset allocation targets and acceptable ranges within each asset class

   b. Portfolio return objectives

   c. Investment authority: Who can execute trades on your behalf and what, if any, communication is required or desired for this

   d. Investment execution: Preferences for investment vehicles to use, restrictions on speed of cash being invested, and transition plan guidelines to move to the recommended portfolio

2. Definition of overall investment parameters to help manage risk in the portfolio. These may include the following sub-elements:

    a. Investment time horizon: Time until you need cash flow and your life expectancy

    b. Liquidity requirements: Cash or near-cash needs

    c. Tax sensitivity: How much tax to realize in any year and updated tax brackets (both state and federal)

    d. Risk tolerance (the amount of market correction you can tolerate without making an emotional decision to sell) and the measurement of portfolio risk

    e. Restrictions: Stocks to hold, stocks to not buy, etc.

    f. Annual and periodic cash flow requirements: Your spending policy

3. Communication of this plan to appropriate parties: Investment managers, other interested family members, accountant/tax person, financial planner, etc.

4. Written strategy and guidelines for handling decisions regarding the management of your portfolio assets. Specifically these may include:

    a. Investment guidelines by asset class, including items such as credit quality, sector weightings, maturities, types of investment instruments used, etc.

    b. Specific security or asset restrictions not included elsewhere in the document

5. Establish a methodology for evaluating performance of the portfolio. Address issues such as:

    a. Overall portfolio benchmark (an index, or indices, against which you can gauge how well or poorly your portfolio is performing versus a basket of similar investments) tied to the return objective

    b. Benchmarks for individual portfolio components

    c. Timeframe over which to evaluate the performance and acceptable variances to the benchmark

    d. Tradeoffs between risk and return to potentially increase or decrease the likelihood of meeting or exceeding your return objective

Investment plans are often evaluated by how well the investor is doing relative to standard industry benchmarks. Yet, many investors do not want to measure the success of their plans in that manner. I will cover this in more detail in Chapter 13.

After you create this IPS, what are you supposed to do with it? Quite simply, you want to share it with everyone who has a need to know. This was my point in number three above. Share the IPS with your current circle of trusted advisors, whether that is a small circle that includes your accountant and your broker, or a larger circle that includes money managers, consultants, estate planners, etc.

This is where your left brain—the analytical side—comes in. You should sit down and think about your goals and objectives, your needs, and how you are wired. At the same time, you should assess your situation and your resources, and start the process of developing your investment plan. The exact form of the plan is not important, but it is absolutely critical to go through the exercise to create one. You cannot delegate this to your spouse or to a business partner. The process has value in and of itself because, for many investors, it is the first time they have clearly thought through their goals and objectives in life and how their investments will play a role in that. It may also be the first time that you have discussed these important issues with your spouse or partner.

RIGHT BRAIN: ADDING FUN AND CREATIVITY TO YOUR INVESTMENT PLAN

The right side of the brain is the random, intuitive, holistic, and subjective part of the brain. It is also referred to as the fun and creative part of the brain. Once you develop an overall game plan with the analytical side of your brain, it is time to switch to the creative side. This is where you can incorporate some fun and creativity into your portfolio, or at least give it some consideration.

Fun and creativity in your portfolio can take many different forms and not distract from your overall plan. That is a key factor here. For many investors, actually implementing the investment plan will depend, to some degree, on how interesting the process is. Many investors have good intentions, but they get bored too easily. There are other fun or more pressing issues to attend to—or so they think!

Let's look at it another way. Take working out, for example. In the ongoing quest to keep your body in shape, boredom can often become a hurdle. After a while, you get bored with the same exercise routines, and that is where sticking to the discipline becomes difficult. Personal trainers often advise clients to mix it up—to get out of their everyday routines—and try a different form of exercise to provide their bodies with the same benefit, but in a different way. Like hiring a personal trainer, you can also hire an investment advisor to help you on your investment journey. I will talk about how to go about finding a qualified advisor in Chapter 15.

The Brain and Investing

Now let's explore some examples of right brain investing. Many investors hold individual stocks as part of their portfolios. One way to inject some fun into the process is to invest in the companies that make the products you buy or consume on a regular basis. Maybe it is a retailer you frequently visit for your day-to-day needs, or a consumer products company that makes products you use. It's okay to incorporate some of these into your portfolio as long as the investments meet all the other criteria important in analyzing investments.

Figure 9

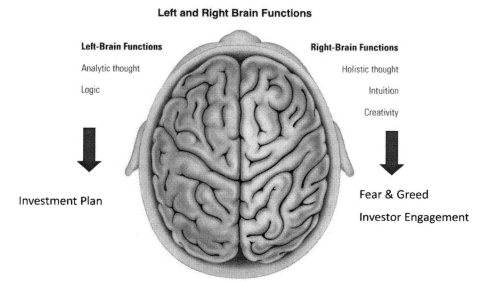

Left and Right Brain Functions

Left-Brain Functions

Analytic thought

Logic

Investment Plan

Right-Brain Functions

Holistic thought

Intuition

Creativity

Fear & Greed

Investor Engagement

Source: Author Analysis

Another way to notch up the interest level is to carry this concept across asset categories. I was talking about stocks in the example I just provided. You could also do the same thing with bonds. In municipal bond land, you could buy bonds in your local school district or general obligation bonds of the city in which you live (keeping proper diversification in mind).

In the real estate asset category, you could purchase an ownership interest in an office building or an apartment complex in the city where you live, or better yet, a piece of property in another city for geographic diversification. Some investors get satisfaction and enjoyment from periodically driving by a piece of property they own and literally seeing their investment.

It is important not to carry this concept too far, though. I have seen investors who end up concentrated in just a couple of economic sectors, or with a geographic concentration by following this approach. That usually does not lead to long-term investment success. The reason is that economic problems in one city can often spread across businesses and properties within that city, thereby impacting many of your seemingly diversified investments if they are concentrated in that local market.

Another way to add some fun to your investing journey is simply by learning. There is an abundance of opportunities to acquire books or read about individual investment topics and the investment process on the Internet. Discover what interests you. Many investment firms and/or advisors also conduct seminars that are often educational and done in a setting that makes it enjoyable to learn. Investment clubs were very popular in the bull market of the 1980s and 1990s. However, their numbers dramatically reduced after the bear market that followed. In spite of their diminished popularity, they can still be a way to combine creativity with an investment learning experience, as well as a social outlet.

I know some folks who attend annual meetings and conferences as a way to make investing fun. Some say the ultimate annual meeting is the Berkshire Hathaway meeting in Omaha, Nebraska. Hosted by legendary investor Warren Buffett, this event is a pilgrimage of sorts for many investors seeking to have fun, yet who also want to learn from the master investor himself. Other investors attend annual meetings simply to get the freebies. This can be both informative and fun—learning more about what is happening at the company and snagging free samples of company products at the same time.

When you attend an annual company meeting, you can learn a lot about the company's products. In addition, there is the possibility that you will get an update on existing products that are selling well, and even hear about new products that hold promise for the future. You may also hear a basic vision or company game plan, but beyond that you will likely not get much else—such as whether or not the company represents a good investment. You need to be cautious in getting too excited about a charismatic chief executive officer (CEO) who can spin a great story and may be a fantastic speaker. Sometimes CEOs use their charisma and public speaking skills to mask companies in which you should not invest. On the flipside, there is the potential to miss out on a good opportunity from time to time because the CEO is not very compelling because of a lack of upfront presentation skills.

Some families participate in investment retreats at resort-type locations to go over their family portfolios, share investment values, and also spend a lot of quality time together. The organizers of these retreats often bring in professional investment experts, planners, and legal professionals to go through various aspects of investors' wealth over the course of a couple of days.

ANOTHER RIGHT BRAIN CONSIDERATION: FEAR AND GREED

Warren Buffett said it best when he said, "Be fearful when others are greedy and greedy when others are fearful." I will cover some of this in other sections of the book, but my basic advice here is to avoid letting your emotions dictate your investment plans. In many respects, the market has a herd mentality. When one person starts selling, others begin to follow. Soon you can have a selling panic, largely driven by fear.

The flipside of this can also be dangerous, and it leads to what I like to call a "buying panic." This is where investors worry about missing out on the great bull market and start piling into stocks, often hoping for large gains in relatively short periods of time. My advice is to take as much emotion out of the investment process as possible. Maybe you need to switch back to the left brain style of analytical and logical thinking in order to refocus. It may mean ignoring what your friends bought that suddenly went up substantially—or that they say went up. It may also be a good idea to turn off the news when fear is in the air. (We will discuss the notion of filtering information in Chapter 6.)

Healthy Investment Tips

1. Develop an investment plan and document that plan in your IPS.
2. Review the IPS annually to ensure it is still appropriate for you. Only make changes if your life situation has changed or investment allocations need to be updated.
3. Add some fun, creativity, and learning into your investment journey.
4. Avoid the extremes of fear and greed.

5

The Eyes: Investing by Looking Forward

Eyes: Organs of vision or of light sensitivity

Our eyes are in the front of our heads for a reason: so we can look forward to where we are going. If our eyes were placed in the back of our heads, then arguably we would spend a lot of time looking backward. This is an important principle in investing—the discipline of looking forward rather than backward.

Many investors must have eyes in the back of their heads. I come to this conclusion because their investment decisions seem to be made while they are looking backward. They look backward at historical performance data when picking funds or managers, and yet there is little predictive value in doing so. Some investors also look backward in picking areas of the market or industries that have done well. Notice I used the word "have" here. This is a different proposition than trying to find investments that will or may do well in the future.

A lot of folks experience difficulty with their vision and are often either categorized as being near-sighted or far-sighted. Near-sighted people can see great close-up, but would not be able to see the centerfielder in a baseball game from home plate without corrective vision. Those who are far-sighted can see well far away, but not so well close-up.

Figure 10   Rearview Mirror

In the investment world, it is important to look forward (or ahead) both at the near and at the far away. Having a strategy for dealing with tomorrow, while also planning for ten years down the road, is more intertwined than many investors realize. The classic example of this revolves around risk, and specifically, the ability of the investor to tolerate various levels of risk. An investor may have a perfectly allocated portfolio that, over a long period of time, will have a very high probability of meeting his or her goals. However, if it is too risky and dealing with the day-to-day volatility is unsettling for the investor, the portfolio will likely fail. The reason for this is that the investor will likely bail out of the plan at the first sign of trouble or dip in the market, thereby nixing its ability to work over the long run. A bailed plan is a failed plan.

The ability to tolerate short-term volatility for long-term benefit revolves around something I call "the smoothness of the ride." If, as an investor, you have a portfolio that provides a relatively smooth ride (e.g., low volatility), you will be more likely to stick with your long-term plan and not bail out at the absolute worst time. I have seen investors who theoretically have the ability to be positioned for long-term growth in their portfolios, but bail out in a market downturn. By doing this, they essentially mess up their entire investment plans. It's better to structure your portfolio a little less aggressively and with broader diversification to allow yourself a higher probability of sticking with your plan and meeting your long-term goal. See the chart below that shows how a smooth ride can benefit an investor's portfolio over time.

Figure 11 Smoothness of the Ride

Performance of Three Hypothetical Portfolios

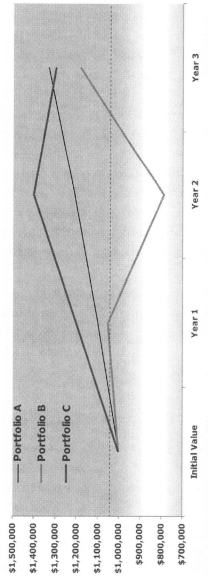

	Portfolio A	Portfolio B	Portfolio C
Year 1	10%	5%	20%
Year 2	10%	-25%	20%
Year 3	10%	50%	-10%
Total Arithmetic Return	30%	30%	30%
Ending Value	$1,331,000	$1,181,250	$1,296,000

In Figure 11, you can see dramatic differences between three different port-folios that have the same arithmetic average return over a three-year period. The key is not the average, but the *range* of possible returns in any given year. Clearly, a smooth ride for an investor is dependent to a large degree on reducing the drawdown impact. The way the math works, it simply takes a much bigger return to recover from a loss than what the percentage of the loss would indicate. For example, a 50 percent portfolio drawdown requires a 100 percent gain to get back to even.

A great example of how the math of the smoothness of the ride can work out is from the 2008–2009 U.S. equity bear market. The peak to trough drop in the market was 57 percent, which would take a 133 percent return to recover back to even. Had an investor been invested in a well-diversified, multi-asset class portfolio during that bear market, it may have been down about 25 percent peak to trough. A 25 percent decline requires a 33 percent return to recover to even. This is a 100 percent return difference to recover and illustrates the value of diversification in a difficult investment environment.

In the example of Portfolio B, the whole issue is further complicated by an investor who may not bail out at the bottom, but who gets considerably more conservative at the bottom of the market. This action will likely result in the portfolio's expected return being reset at a lower level, thereby resulting in an even longer period of time to recoup the losses.

OPTICAL ILLUSION: THE INVESTOR STARTS SEEING THINGS

The optical illusion is one of the least understood, yet most dangerous problems faced by investors. Most forms of this problem can be isolated into four distinct stages, or scenes, if you want to think of it as a short film. So let's switch gears from learning about anatomy for a bit and watch a short film called *The Investment Follies.*

Before I get into the four scenes, let me first explain the phrase, "investment follies." Simply put, investment follies are the investor's quest to find a good investment based exclusively on historical data, or performance. This quest leads to actions that have a detrimental impact on the investor's long-term performance, as evidenced by Figure 12.

Figure 12   Returns for Stock Investors from 1990 to 2010

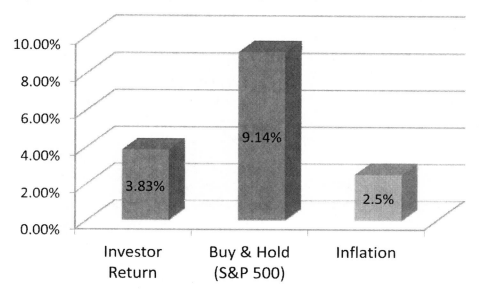

This chart describes actual investor returns over a twenty-year timeframe, undoubtedly impacted to a great extent by common investment follies. The notion of investor return is important because this is the actual return earned by investors. This is not some model performance or fund performance record that very few investors may have actually achieved. This is the return the investor actually received; you may need to visualize the film script that follows to understand why.

An additional analysis on investor behavior was done by The Leuthold Group. It analyzed investor flows of money into and out of mutual funds, and found that investors tended to buy stocks when valuations were close to twenty times earnings and sell stocks when valuations were a little more than fifteen times earnings—in other words, buying high and selling low.

Scene One: Enlightenment

The first scene is what I call *Enlightenment*. During this scene, the investor finds an investment that has done so well that everyone is talking about it.

Investors are rushing to put money into this investment because it is clearly something everyone needs in their portfolios. Investors think that if they miss out, there will certainly be regret over this missed opportunity.

After the investor joins the other investors and places money into this investment, it continues to do well for a time, only reinforcing what a very smart decision this was. Then, the tide changes, and the investment suddenly starts to do poorly. The enlightened investor is not worried, fortified by the knowledge of past excellent returns. In fact, the enlightened investor has read that if an investment goes down, one should take advantage of that and buy the dips. So the enlightened investor buys more.

As more time passes, and the investment continues to do poorly, the enlightened investor becomes cautious and does not buy more. Instead, the investor decides to hold on to the investment.

Scene Two: Disenchantment

The second scene is called *Disenchantment.* Even more time has passed, and the investment continues to do poorly. The once-enlightened investor becomes disenchanted and starts looking for a new investment. The disenchanted investor follows the same process to enlightenment as was done in choosing the first investment. The investor begins to look for investments that have done really well (emphasis on "have done").

Not surprisingly, the investor finds such an investment. Not only has it done well historically, but it has also done well recently—unlike the prior investment. The disenchanted investor sells the original investment and buys the new investment.

Scene Three: Nirvana

The disenchanted investor now enters scene three, *Nirvana.* The investor finally feels very good about how things are going. The investor has been tested after having picked a bad investment, found a better one, and then got rid of the first one, and is wiser for the whole experience. Right?

The answer must be yes, the investor would say. After all, the new investment is doing exceptionally well. The investment is going up seemingly every day. This has caused the investor to share information about the investment with relatives and friends, and more investors rush to buy this investment, causing it to go up even more.

However, something invariably happens that causes the investment to switch directions and start to fall. The investor still believes and buys more on the dip. But it continues to fall and the investor starts to worry, not adding anything else. The investor holds the position. More days pass and the investment continues to drop. Suddenly, the investor hopes that relatives and friends *didn't* buy any of the investment.

Scene Four: Rewind

The fourth and final scene is called *Rewind*. I call this scene *Rewind* because the whole process starts over now. The investor searches for a new investment, and after finding one, exits from the second investment. Invariably, at about this same time, the original investment the investor purchased back in the *Enlightened* scene starts to go back up again, which really confuses the investor after having kept track of it since selling (which many investors do for some reason).

Notice the pattern in Figure 13.

THE INVESTMENT FOLLIES: FIVES LESSONS

1. Investors often chase historical performance, which has little predictive value for future performance.

Figure 13 Investment Follies: Four Scenes

Scene	How Does it Start?	How Does it End?
Enlightenment	Finding a great past performer	Current performance disappoints
Disenchantment	Current performance disappoints	Finding a great past & present performer
Nirvana	Finding a great past & present performer	Current performance disappoints
Rewind	Repeat the process	

Source: Author Analysis

Figure 14   Past Performance is a Poor Guide to Future Performance

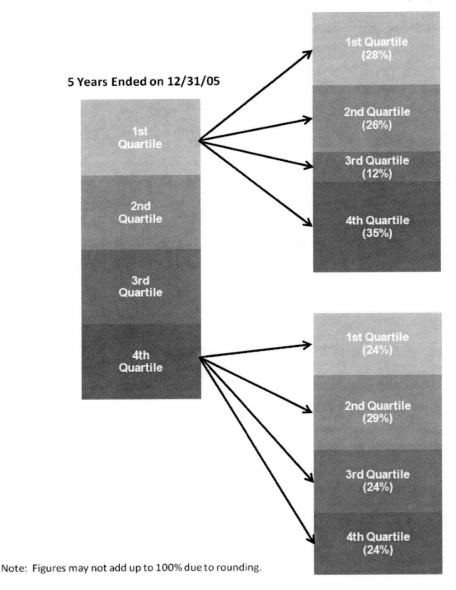

Note: Figures may not add up to 100% due to rounding.

Source: RogersCasey, June 2011

Figure 14 illustrates this idea by using fund returns at the end of 2000 in the large-cap core (large company stock finds that have no particular style bias) area and then looking at those same managers five years later.

What this data shows is that more of the top-quartile managers in 2005 went to the bottom of the pack by the end of five years than stayed in the top group. On the flipside, an equal percentage of the fourth quartile managers from 2005 moved into the top group as stayed in the bottom group.

2. Investors often unknowingly chase hot asset classes or styles and then pick the hottest manager in that category. Do not look at a list of top-performing mutual funds at any given point in time and then conclude that they are worthy of purchase. It is highly likely that if you pick the top three funds over, let's say, a three-year time period, those three funds will all be investing in similar things. In other words, you will not get the diversification you think you should have by buying three different funds.

3. Investors often mistake a poor-performing manager for an asset class or style that is simply out of favor. Invariably, this leads them to sell out at a market trough.

4. Buying the hottest of the hot managers sets up investors for a double whammy. If an investor buys the asset class or style close to its peak, and then picks the manager that did best ascending the peak, that manager will likely fall the fastest as it comes off the peak.

5. The triple whammy occurs when the investment that is sold comes off its trough and starts its cyclical ascension to the peak.

In a very interesting study done by Litman/Gregory Research in 2006, the group found that most managers that have a ten-year track record of outperforming the market have a three-year period of time when they underperform the market by at least 2 percentage points a year. Selling that manager during one of those three-year underperformance periods can result in selling a top manager that is just going through a tough performance patch that nearly every manager goes through. Figure 15 highlights some of the findings of the group's research.

Figure 15 Patience Can Have Its Rewards

Managers who outperform in the long run may under perform for short periods

	Large Blend	Large Growth	Large Value
Percentage of funds that trailed for three years by at least 2% annualized	94%	93%	100%
Percentage of funds that trailed for three years by at least 5% annualized	71%	68%	64%

Source: Litman/Gregory Asset Management, LLC, September 2006. Reprinted with permission

HOW TO AVOID THE INVESTMENT FOLLIES

My guidance for avoiding the investment follies is as follows:

1. Implement a rigorous asset allocation framework by avoiding the overload of in-favor asset classes or styles. In other words, make sure you are truly diversified and don't just own several funds or managers that do the same thing.

2. Use institutional quality due diligence that looks beyond historical returns. Qualitative factors can be more predictive in finding funds or managers that will do well going forward.

3. Continuously pursue education of the investment process and key investment principles. This can give you a better chance for investment success.

4. Stick with a manager going through short-term market underperformance. This will help you avoid getting whipsawed.

5. Focus on overall portfolio performance rather than individual components.

6. Use an advisor with experience actually managing money—one who understands that styles go in and out of favor.

Simply put, by maintaining your investment focus and sticking to the principles outlined above, you can avoid the investment follies and better position yourself to meet your long-term investment objectives.

Healthy Investment Tips

1. Always remember to look forward, not backward. Spend more time thinking about what will work in the environment we have now and will likely have in the future rather than what worked well in the past.
2. Structure your portfolio for a smooth ride. This will help to keep you from throwing in the towel if the markets get challenging.
3. Drawdown is one of the biggest risks individual investors face. Make sure your investment plan takes this into account. Hint: Investments that have big, outsized gains can also have big, outsized losses that can be tough to recover from.
4. Exercise patience and discipline in sticking with your investment plan.

6

The Ears: Listening Selectively and Avoiding Investment Information Overload

Ears: Organs of hearing; responsible for maintaining equilibrium as well as sensing sound

Generally, the ears are designed for listening. It is not often that I am accused of listening too much, yet in the investment world, that can actually be dangerous. I am referring to information overload. Information overload is essentially being exposed to volumes of information and data but then being unable to process it to arrive at a logical conclusion or plan of action.

WHERE DO YOU GET ADVICE?

Figure 16 shows that investors get advice from a variety of sources in addition to their investment advisor, including daily financial press, cable TV, financial advisor or financial provider websites, and other websites focused specifically on investing. In Figure 16, an affluent investor is defined as someone with more than $500,000 of investable assets. An ultra high net worth (UHNW) investor is an investor with $5 million or more of investable assets.

Figure 16 Where Do Investors Get Advice

	Affluent Investor %	UHNW Investor %
Primary Financial Advisor	31%	52%
Daily Financial Press	9%	22%
Cable Television	10%	9%
Web sites other than Advisor/Provider	19%	8%
Advisor/Provider Web site	10%	6%

Data Source: Spectrum Group 2/11.

We all know that listening is important when it comes to hearing the needs and goals of our family members. What is important to them? What goals do they have? What shared goals do you have as a family? This may take the form of a second home or a shared interest in a charity or some other philanthropic desire.

Listening is also important when it comes to creating a circle of trusted advisors and experts who can advise you and your family. It is important to hear what they have to say and to create opportunities or a forum to regularly receive that advice. The information and ideas your advisors provide can be important as you implement and execute your investment plan.

Information overload, or what I also refer to as investment sensory overload, is a big problem for many investors. The advent of electronic media has made it easy to access huge amounts of information on a wide range of investment topics. We also live in a complex global economy with sophisticated financial markets influenced by a whole host of factors. Various pieces of data on these factors come out daily, and sometimes multiple times a day. These data points are then reported on, commented on, pontificated about, and analyzed and reanalyzed every single day.

There is also a human reactional bias to negative information. What I mean by this is that we tend to react more significantly to negative information than we do to positive information. Numerous studies have shown that individuals react as much as 30 percent more powerfully to negative information than equally positive information. The media understand this negative bias, and as a result, you will likely hear about more tragedies than triumphs, even though they may be more balanced in reality. This can cause us to think that things are worse than they are and impact our investment decision-making process. This is another reason why we should be careful in filtering the flow of negative news we consume.

I do not believe that the mere presence of mounds of information will necessarily make you a better investor. In fact, too much information can make it that much more difficult to figure out what to do. This seems to be a growing problem for investors. The proliferation of information has made many investors confused and anxious rather than more certain in their investment strategy.

Another related problem is the frequent checking of performance and portfolio values. If you check the performance of your stocks, mutual funds, ETFs, and other investments on a daily basis, *stop it!* If, for some reason, you check the prices of your investments multiple times per day, find a hobby! Typically, there is no information in the daily price movement of your investments that you should act on (unless you are attempting to be a day trader, which I strongly advise against). Furthermore, there are likely no lifestyle changes that you should make based on the daily valuation of your portfolio. Checking performance and portfolio values daily may take your eye off what is really important—the long-term performance of your portfolio relative to your individual goals.

Filtering the Flow of Information

What, then, is an investor to do? Here are a few tips on how to screen the investment information you utilize:

1. **Turn off the flow of information.** I know people who constantly have business and market news programs on their televisions. There are simply too many people with too many opinions on too many topics that change day to day for you to develop any sort of rationale approach listening to this. Look at your programming guide. If there is a show that has a guest you are interested in, then tune in; otherwise, tune out. If you are familiar with the phrases "in one ear and out the other" or "turn a deaf ear to what was said," this may be the time to put them in action.

2. **Use a knowledgeable, experienced advisor.** Be clear with the advisor on what role you want him or her to play and how much you want to hear from that advisor. Your advisor can be effective in keeping you disciplined when you are hearing multiple views on the markets on a daily basis. Your advisor can also act as an information filter for you, which can be very helpful in reducing the amount of information to which you need access.

3. **Schedule periodic portfolio review sessions.** Continually evaluating your portfolio based on the daily flow of information can be hazardous to your wealth (and possibly your health). Discipline yourself to look at your portfolio periodically—schedule a quarterly review, for example—and gather information for a week or ten days before the review that can help you when you sit down for that review. This review will likely be most effective if you do it with the help of your advisor.

The Portfolio Review

What should happen in the portfolio review? Many investors and advisors think it is just going over past performance. They think of it is an investment report card, if you will. That is certainly one of the items that should be reviewed, but not the only one—and likely not the most important. What, then, should you review? Take a look at this checklist for potential portfolio review agenda items:

1. *How am I doing?* This is not just past performance. This is how you are doing relative to your goals. It is a check back to see how you are tracking

to achieve your goals that should have been established as part of your investment plan.

2. *What, if anything, has changed in my life since the last review? Does that have an impact on my investment plan?* If so, explore adjustments that need to be made to your plan and then translate those adjustments to your portfolio.

3. *Has my asset allocation veered far enough away from my target allocation to require rebalancing?* If so, this would be a time when you could put your rebalancing plan into action.

4. *Are your asset classes and weightings working together as you had planned?* If not, explore if this is due to market conditions or to a manager straying from his or her process. If it is due to market conditions, do nothing. If it is due to a manager not doing what he or she said he or she was going to do, ask some tough questions and explore other potential managers. Make sure that you do not fire a manager for a short-term performance miss that had nothing to do with a change in his or her process.

5. *Is this portfolio and investment plan allowing you to sleep at night?* In other words, is the risk profile correct? If not, consider adjusting, as appropriate.

Whether you are doing a self-review of your portfolio or using an advisor to do a review with you, I suggest using an agenda for the meeting. This will help you (and/or your advisor) to stay focused on the review meeting and ensure that you cover all of the important elements of the review. If you are using an advisor, I suggest you ask the advisor to periodically include a section on new ideas for the portfolio. This could include your updated shopping list of items that you want to add to the portfolio at some point and at a certain price. (Note that this will be discussed in more detail in the next section of this book.)

I would also ask your advisor to periodically include a section in the review meeting to educate you on some area of the investment world that you know little about. I would focus on an area that could conceivably become a part of your investment portfolio in the future or that is a consideration due to the investment planning process. This could be a wealth management concept, such as the use of estate planning techniques in your overall investment plan.

Healthy Investment Tips

1. Turn off information overload to avoid the risk of getting too much information or feeling like you need to constantly make decisions regarding your portfolio.
2. If information overload is a problem, use an experienced advisor to help you stay on track and manage the flow of information you receive.
3. Review your portfolio regularly and ask relevant questions that matter using the checklist provided in this chapter.
4. Be careful in your response to what is likely to be a bias toward more negative information than positive.

7

The Nose: Sniffing Out the Impact of Your Investment Environment

Nose: The forward part of the head that contains the organs of smell and the beginning of the respiratory tract; used to smell or sniff

Developing a sense of smell, so to speak, can be important in your investment life. Often this is referred to as "passing the smell test." As an investor, you will hear and read about a lot of ideas that will not seem quite right—in other words, they just don't smell right. More often than not, following your nose is good advice.

One example of a bad smell is anything that appears to offer returns much higher than other investments within the same category. If it sounds too good to be true, it probably is worth avoiding. Another example is an investment that carries disproportionate risk to the return. You may get a great return, but only if a lot of things work out right—and work out right simultaneously.

The nose can also be valuable in sniffing out bad odors emanating from investments that already exist in the portfolio. These are investments that went bad a long time ago, but emotionally, the investor is having a hard time throwing away. In other situations, there may not be a specific problem with the investment, but no one is following it. If the investment is not being followed and analyzed, it should probably be sold. Stock spin-offs often fall into this category. These are often divisions of large companies that are distributed to shareholders as a separate company—with it's own stock. In many cases, there is nothing wrong with these, and you may have even intended to clean them up (code for sell), but you have just not gotten around to it. In any event, these spin-offs are being ignored; you should just sell them if that is the case.

The nose can also be useful in sniffing out opportunities that the market and the economy present to us. Contrarian investing is a good example of this. Contrarian investors tend to look for opportunities in the market that are unloved, or at least under-loved. This could be a sector of the market on which everyone is negative (most likely because it has been a weak performer). It could also mean a specific company or an asset class that is out of favor.

Patient investors can sometimes find excellent long-term opportunities by carefully allowing some contrarian ideas into their portfolios. The phrase, "nose into this area," meaning proceed with caution, is good advice for investors who participate in contrarian investing because it requires diligent research and a lot of patience.

The economy can also offer you investment opportunities, but your nose will have to be calibrated to separate the false smells from the real ones. If you want to simplify your analysis of the economy, divide it into four sectors: consumer, business, government, and prices and valuation. There is an abundance of data gathered and reported on almost every week on each of these sectors. Most of it you should ignore. Why? Read on.

GARBAGE AND OPPORTUNITIES

In the consumer sector, it's all about jobs. If consumers have jobs, they will spend money; therefore, the consumer sector will likely be in good shape. Look at the unemployment rate. Historically, if the unemployment rate has been below 5 percent, the economy is experiencing full employment. What this means is that most everyone who wants a job and has the skills needed in the current economy can find one, and that represents a good environment for the consumer part of the economy.

Strategists, economists, and the financial media look at and report on a whole host of other data on the consumer. However, most of it is noise and not worth your time analyzing. As the economy has gone through a significant transformation in the last few years, the long-term unemployment rate has increased significantly. This may result in the "full employment" level being higher than the 5 percent for the next several years as we work through the changes required in the workforce.

In the business sector, it is not as simple. There are two key indicators you should look at. The first one is earnings growth. Are companies growing their earnings at a reasonable pace? Generally, reaching above 10 percent annually is a constructive environment. The second indicator to look at is revenue growth. Are companies growing their revenue—also referred to as their top-line growth (in contrast to the bottom line, which represents earnings growth)—by at least 7 percent annually?

Your nose needs to be on guard for companies growing their bottom line, but not their top line. This could be a red flag that they are financial engineering their earnings growth without the benefit of real business growth. The financial engineering could come in many forms. Some ways can be easy to understand, such as basic cost-cutting, and others are more difficult to understand—most notably, accounting gimmickry.

In the government sector, you could pay attention to the Federal Reserve, also known as the Fed. In fact, media stories about the Fed are very prevalent. What is the Fed going to do? Will it raise interest rates or lower them? If you are bored and have a lot of time on your hands, it may be interesting to try and guess what the Fed is going to do. Alternatively, you could just spend more time with your family and simply look at the yields of the six-month Treasury bill and the ten-year Treasury note every now and then. These yields reflect what is going on with interest rates in our economy, which impact both consumers and businesses.

Another item you could look at is the government budget deficit. The sheer size of the number will likely depress you, so I would not spend too much time looking at this. The market does not care much about the month-to-month numbers. The trend, however, is worth looking at from time to time to see if the deficit is trending higher or lower and what impact this could have on government bond issuance and interest rates.

In addition to government budget deficits, at the time of this book revision, there is considerable debate about the future reach of government in the U.S.

After spending huge amounts of money for stimulus programs to combat the recession of 2008 and 2009, and increased spending for new social programs, the government now makes up a bigger portion of the economy than it did ten years ago. This comes at a time when European economies are trying to figure out how to scale back the size of government, bring deficits down, and restore confidence in their currencies and markets. As such, investors may need to pay even more attention to this part of the economy in the future.

The prices and valuation sector is important. What is happening with inflation is important to you as an investor, and you should pay attention to that. Inflation impacts your purchasing power and can erode the value of your portfolio over time. It impacts your bond portfolio and your cash inflow or, most prominently, your cash outflow. On the valuation side, you should look at the prices-to-earnings ratio of stocks. If the market is much higher than twenty—meaning that you are paying $20 for every $1 of earnings, or what is referred to in the market as a 5 percent earnings yield (one divided by twenty)—you should be careful. If the market gets below fifteen, you should get interested. These are gross oversimplifications because many factors are at play here, but this at least gives you some sense of valuations.

BULL OR BEAR?

If you're just starting out as an investor, you may be wondering, *What is a bear market? A bull market? A correction? Should I care about any of this? If so, what should I do if I find myself in one of these markets?* Simply put, a **bear market** is generally considered to be a market that is down 20 percent or more from its high. A **bull market** is generally considered to be a market that is up 20 percent or more from its past high. A **correction** is generally considered to be a market that is down 10 percent or more from its recent high. It is common for the market to experience frequent corrections within a bull market, yet not get as severe as a bear market.

Take a look at the following diagrams. Figure 17 shows the bear markets in this country since the 1920s, including their duration and the severity of the decline. Figure 18 shows the bull markets in this country since 1920, including their duration and the percentage increase.

Figure 17   Bear Markets: Dow Jones Industrial Average (DJIA)

Peak Date	Trough Date	Duration in Months	Percent Decline
9/3/1929	7/8/1932	34.1	-87.19%
9/7/1932	2/27/1933	5.7	-37.25%
7/18/1933	10/21/1933	3.1	-23.03%
2/5/1934	7/26/1934	5.6	-22.76%
3/10/1937	4/26/1942	61.6	-52.20%
5/29/1946	6/13/1949	36.5	-23.95%
12/13/1961	6/26/1962	6.4	-27.10%
2/9/1966	5/26/1970	51.5	-36.58%
1/11/1973	12/6/1974	22.6	-45.06%
9/21/1976	2/28/1978	17.3	-26.87%
4/27/1981	8/12/1982	15.5	-24.13%
8/25/1987	10/19/1987	1.8	-36.13%
7/17/1990	10/11/1990	2.8	-21.16%
1/14/2000	10/9/2002	32.8	-37.85%
10/9/2007	3/9/2009	17	-53.78

Data Source: Bloomberg Finance. L.P., 2011.

Figure 18   Bull Markets: DJIA

Trough Date	Peak Date	Duration in Years	Percent Increase
8/24/1921	9/3/1929	8	496.50%
7/8/1932	9/7/1932	0.2	93.90%
2/27/1933	7/18/1933	0.4	116.60%
10/21/1933	2/5/1934	0.3	32.40%
7/26/1934	3/10/1937	2.6	127.30%
4/28/1942	5/29/1946	4.1	128.70%
6/13/1949	12/13/1961	12.5	354.80%
6/26/1962	2/9/1966	3.6	85.70%
5/26/1970	1/11/1973	2.6	66.60%
12/8/1974	9/21/1976	1.8	75.70%
2/28/1978	4/27/1981	3.2	38.00%
8/12/1982	8/25/1987	5	250.40%
10/19/1987	7/17/1990	2.7	72.50%
10/11/1990	1/14/2000	9.3	395.70%
10/9/2002	10/9/2007	5	94.4%

Source: Bloomberg Finance, L.P., 2011

As an investor, you need to be aware of the type of market environment you are in because each of these environments will present you with opportunities and dangers. The overriding principle you need to think about in each of these environments is to keep your emotions in check. Don't get too excited and start ignoring risks when the market is in a bull phase. On the flipside, don't get too depressed and throw in the towel when the market is in a bear phase. Furthermore, don't veer from your investment plan in a correction phase of a market.

This leads me to the second thing an investor should do in each of these markets—*stick to your long-term plan!* Investors have the tendency to question their long-term plans when they find themselves in an emotional market environment—either bull or bear. In a bull market, investors tend to believe they are possibly being too conservative; after all, in a bull market those who take the greatest risks often reap the biggest rewards. In a bear market, investors think they have been too aggressive; higher-risk investments get pounded the hardest in that environment.

Sticking to your long-term plan does not mean doing nothing. It may be appropriate to dial up or dial down risk by making adjustments to allocations to different asset categories in the portfolio. Also, there may be changes that make sense in the portfolio composition with specific investments that are better suited for the market environment at the time, but these changes are all within the framework of the long-term plan. At the risk of being redundant, I say again, stick with your plan!

The following list is a good reminder for investors.

LESSONS LEARNED IN A BEAR MARKET

- Question everything.
- There are no gurus.
- Pay attention to early red flags.
- If it looks too good to be true, *run!*
- Do the math yourself; if the company says two plus two equals six, trust your own numbers.

- Don't trust backward-looking quant models that found a formula for the past that may or may not work in the future.
- Too much leverage can turn a modest problem into a catastrophe.
- Pay attention to economic drivers that will often impact areas of your portfolio that you had not thought about.
- Conventional wisdom learning during a bull market is of minimal value in a bear market.
- Pay attention to valuation and pinch yourself when you see analysts regularly raising price targets.
- Pay attention to starting valuation. At the time that you invest, if valuations are much higher than long-term averages, the potential downside risk is often higher.
- Don't just talk diversification, *do* it! Rebalance regularly and pay some taxes if you need to.
- Be wary of companies that have CEOs with inflated egos (some are now in jail).
- If the market is telling you something, listen.
- Never forget what the money is for when building an investment portfolio.
- Know the importance of strong relationships with your advisors.
- Remember the wise words of Warren Buffett: "Be fearful when others are greedy and greedy when others are fearful."
- There is no birthright that today's market leader will be tomorrow's market leader. The same is true for companies and countries.
- Companies that compromise ethics will eventually be exposed.
- Understand the importance of balance in life.

If you find yourself in a bull market, pull out this list and check to see if any of these bullet points are ringing true. If a number of them are, take it as a warning sign that there may be an eventual end to the upward trend. If you are in a bear market, you will wish you had paid attention to this list when you were in a bull market.

Healthy Investment Tips

1. If it doesn't pass the smell test, or if it sounds too good to be true, avoid it.
2. Patient investors can make money by finding investments that are unloved or under-loved. This is known as contrarian investing.
3. The economic cycle can provide investment opportunities if you know what key factors to look for.
4. Bull and bear markets provide challenges and opportunities for the investor.

8

The Mouth and Stomach: Investment Portion Size and the Four Basic Food Groups of Investments

Mouth: The body opening to take in food; the source of sounds and speech

Stomach: One of the principle organs for the digestion of food

The mouth is the gateway to the stomach. This section is about "feeding" the portfolio. How the portfolio is fed is somewhat dependent on what life stage you are in. If you are relatively young with a long investment horizon in front of you, you will want to keep your portfolio healthy, but growing. If you are older and have a more limited time horizon, you also want a healthy portfolio, but one that is possibly focused more on wealth preservation than on growth.

You learned at an early age that you need four basic food groups to live a healthy life. In your investment portfolio, the four food groups are the four basic asset classes: stocks, bonds, real estate, and alternatives. I think the analogy breaks down if I begin to talk about how many servings of fruits or vegetables you need per day, and try to tie that to an asset class—or does it?

I have seen investors who have the four basic asset classes represented in their portfolios, but who do not succeed because they only had one serving of each. I am talking about diversification within the asset class. If you only have one stock fund, one bond fund, one real estate investment, or one alternative, you run a fairly high risk that some of these funds will not work out that well, thereby negating the benefit of the asset class diversification.

You have probably heard many different people preach about the virtues of taking care of your body—the only one you get. Many investors save diligently and accumulate an impressive amount of wealth. They may do this over a period of time from a stream of income from a successful business or a great job. Alternatively, the wealth could come in one big event like the sale of a business or from an inheritance. Yet, like those who fail to care for their bodies, many investors fail to take good care of their wealth. For many investors, that sum of money they have accumulated will not be recreated in their lifetime if they make poor choices.

For many of us, controlling what we put in our mouths is about balance and portion size. Otherwise, watch out for the stomachache! The same can be said for investors. Often, investors will want what tastes good—and a lot of it. This is played out every day as investors pile into hot investments. If technology stocks are doing well, investors want lots of technology stocks. If real estate is doing well, investors want lots of real estate. Investors will put way too much of their portfolios into these investments, which can lead to balance problems.

In the investment world, the balance problem is solved by diversification. Being properly diversified—even in assets that are not doing very well at the time—is critically important. Avoiding the temptation to sell those assets because they don't taste great, so to speak, and only piling into investments that are very appealing at the present is like throwing out all of your fruits and vegetables and eating only chocolate cake. If you can stick to your investment diet, you will likely avoid many of the stomachaches that invariably come to investors who do not properly balance their portfolios.

This brings us to the most critical decision an investor can make: the asset allocation decision. Figure 19 shows how the variability of investment returns are influenced the most by the asset allocation decision. It is far more important than the individual security decisions or tactical adjustments that you will make in your portfolio. You should spend the appropriate amount of time to make sure you get this right and reevaluate periodically as your life changes.

As Figure 19 illustrates, the strategic asset allocation decision explains 79 percent of a portfolio's variability of returns. Arriving at the correct mix is a combination of art and science. The art part of the answer is driven by your goals; the science part is driven by your risk tolerance.

Investors often misunderstand the amount of risk they can handle in their portfolio. I have found that a useful exercise to get a better handle on risk tolerance is to utilize a risk tolerance questionnaire. Many of the questionnaires that are available online look at risk symmetrically. What this means is that they look at risk from the perspective of opportunity cost or emotional regret of missing out on the benefits of taking on risk. In addition, downside risk is also explored. However, for most individual investors, risk is not symmetrical. Individual investors are often more concerned about the downside risk than the upside opportunity and are willing to trade off some upside opportunity to avoid a big downdraft in their portfolio. A sample risk tolerance questionnaire is included in Appendix VI.

Investors should consider doing a thorough top-to-bottom review of their asset allocation at least once a year, and what better time to do this than at the

Figure 19   Drivers of Investment Portfolio Return Variability

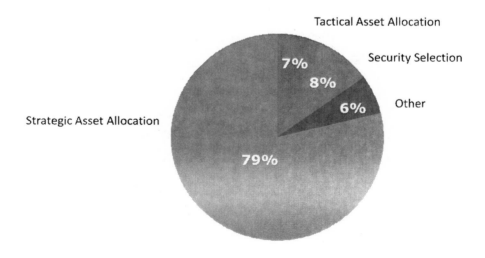

Source: Wells Fargo; "Determinants of Portfolio Returns," 2/10.

beginning of the year? During the financial crisis of 2008 to 2009, many investors made emotional, fear-based decisions relative to their portfolios that may not have been consistent with their long-term investment or life goals. Again, this is a great time to review, recalibrate, and potentially rebalance portfolios to get them back in line with the asset mix that is positioned for your long-term needs.

Take a look at Figure 20. I call this "Dressing in Layers" to help explain and visualize how an investor can review the "layers" of diversification that should be considered in the context of his or her portfolio.

Use these questions to help focus the process:

- **Asset Class:** How am I diversified across asset classes—stocks, bonds, real estate assets, and alternative or complementary strategies?

Figure 20   Dressing in Layers

- **Intra-Asset Class:** How am I diversified within each asset class? For example, how is my tax-exempt bond portfolio diversified by issuer, by state, etc.?

- **Economic Sector:** How is my portfolio diversified relative to economic sectors? For example, do I know how much exposure I have to the U.S. consumer?

- **Income Source:** How is my portfolio diversified by sources of income? For example, how much comes from bond income vs. dividends? How much is dependent on one economic sector?

- **Factor Exposure:** How is my portfolio exposed to and diversified by different economic factors, such as inflation?

- **Policy Exposure:** How is my portfolio exposed and diversified relative to changing government policies?

The answers to these questions should help guide you to changes that may be appropriate for your portfolio.

THE MAJORS AND MINORS

I discussed the importance of asset class diversification and portion size. In this section, I will go over some of the other critical elements of diversification. I want to emphasize that being diversified by major asset class: stocks, bonds, real estate assets, and alternatives is often only the starting point. Intra-asset class diversification, as discussed in this chapter, is very important to investment success in the long-term primarily because it helps smooth out the ride for the investor.

Another way to look at intra-asset class diversification is what I call "the minors." This isn't because they are of minor importance, but because they are often referred to in the industry as "sub-asset classes." Increasingly, investors have a much broader array of sub-asset classes to give them exposure to certain types of assets they previously did not have easy access to. For example, most investors should consider emerging market bond exposure. This would be a sub-asset class (minor) within the bond category. It can be a way for an investor to achieve income source diversification as well as currency diversification in their portfolios—two very important issues for many investors. Neither goals nor risks can be considered in total isolation, much like a doctor would not diagnose a patient by looking only at one side of the patient's body.

For an investor, it is important to understand that the more your assets are scattered among advisors, fund companies, brokerage firms, and so forth, the more difficult it will be to have and maintain a logical asset allocation framework. Make sure that someone is looking at your overall asset allocation—either yourself or your advisor. If your advisor tracks it for you, make sure he or she is objective in how the assets are invested and has no conflict (e.g., higher compensation for different product types that could influence your advisor to tilt it one way or another).

Concentrations are the portion-size problem in the investment world. Investors have a tendency to want a second and third helping of investments that have been recent strong performers. Just because they *have been* strong performers does not mean they *will be.* How often have you wished that you had not had that second or third helping at dinner? Before the investor knows it, he or she has a concentration—and the start of indigestion if anything goes wrong with the investment.

Concentrations are generally considered to be any investment that makes up more than 10 percent of your total portfolio. Concentrations can be very dangerous to your overall investment plan, but can be dealt with in several different ways. I will address concentrations and how to address them in more detail in Chapter 18.

Being disciplined can help solve a lot of the problems of the mouth and stomach. The same is true for investments. Discipline is critically important and often the largest single value an advisor can provide for you—much like a personal trainer who can help keep you on an exercise schedule or a nutritionist who can help you eat right and stay in balance. A good advisor can provide these things and more for your investment portfolio.

Another food analogy that is near and dear to me involves the consumption of junk food. We all know that junk food is bad for us even though it looks appealing and often tastes good. But that initial appeal often leads to a feeling of lethargy. The same can be said for your portfolio if you put too much junk in it. An occasional high-flyer stock probably won't derail your portfolio, but you *will* wonder why you binged on it after it flames out and you are reaching for those antacids. My advice is to avoid the temptation to buy something you hear about from a friend or read about in a magazine unless you have thoroughly read the label.

SENSES NOT COVERED

Earlier in this book, we discussed three of the five senses—seeing, hearing, and smell. We did not dedicate separate chapters to touch and to taste, but they do have important implications for many investors when thinking about their asset allocation.

The sense of touch is important to some investors because they are wired to learn more easily if they can hold or touch an object. A frustration for many investors is that ownership in many investments does not seem to be tangible. The days of even "holding" a paper stock certificate indicating ownership in a company are largely behind us. Many of us do not even get paper statements of our investments as the world continues to go electronic. So even holding a piece of paper that summarizes other pieces of paper indicating ownership is generally going away.

I know many investors who need to hold dirt in their hands and say, "I own this land," or who hold a gold bar to "feel" its weight and know that it is real. To be able to touch a building, walk around in it, and feel its presence is important to many investors, especially those who created wealth in the real estate business. This need for touch or feel has often been an important element of many successful real estate investors. The downside is that it can leave them underexposed to asset classes that simply do not allow this same level of "touch" interaction. Knowing this as an investor can be an important first step in realizing you need other elements to your portfolio.

A good starting point to explore investments without the benefit of touch can be companies where you can at least touch their products. Technology, industrial, consumer, and materials companies all have products that can be touched and can help an investor ease into other important diversifying elements of his or her portfolio.

THE PROBABILITY OF ACHIEVING YOUR GOAL

An important aspect of measuring success that is often overlooked by individual investors is the probability that the portfolios they designed will actually meet their goals. A lot of expected investment-return work is based on historical analysis and averages. In other words, it is based on what has happened in history. On average, you should be *okay* with this approach, but that's not very comforting! There is a better tool you can use; it's called Monte Carlo analysis. Without getting into too much detail, this analysis basically measures the probability that you will meet your goals. This is something you may want to discuss with your advisor, unless you have an online tool that you thoroughly understand that can help you with the math and the analysis of the results.

Figure 21 shows an example of the output of a Monte Carlo analysis on two investors' portfolios. This particular analysis compares and explores the chances (probability) of each portfolio not meeting the investors' goals.

Figure 21　Monte Carlo Analysis

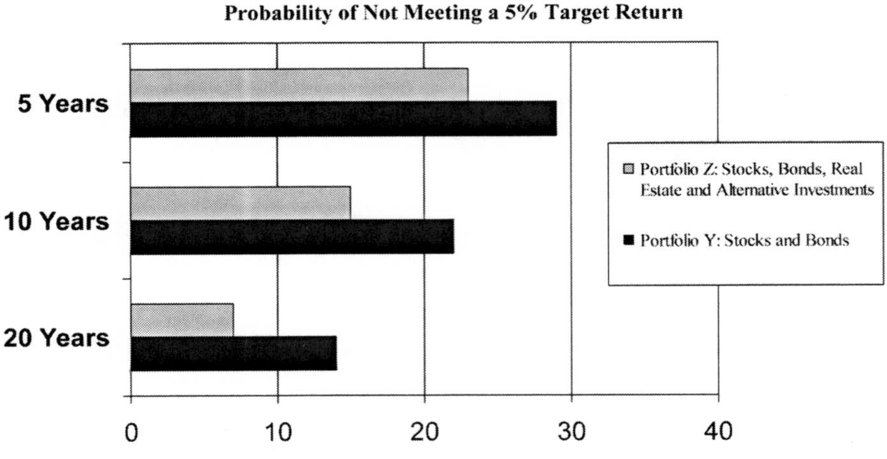

Probability of Not Meeting a 5% Target Return

Portfolio Z: Stocks, Bonds, Real Estate and Alternative Investments

Portfolio Y: Stocks and Bonds

Healthy Investment Tips

1. The asset allocation decision is the most important decision an investor can make.
2. Downside risk, and avoiding a big drawdown, is more important to most individual investors than losing out on an upside opportunity.
3. The more your assets are scattered with various investment providers, the harder it will be to keep track of and manage your asset allocation.
4. Concentrations are a big risk to your portfolio, and you should develop a strategy to deal with them.
5. Discipline is important. Sticking with your investment plan is an important factor in investment success.
6. An important analytical tool that investors can use to determine the probability of meeting (or not meeting) their goals is called Monte Carlo analysis. Ask your advisor for more information about it.

9

The Neck: Portfolio Flexibility

Neck: A connection part that joins the head to the shoulders

The neck is critical to the body in several key ways. (Trust me on this, or try to live without your neck for a day, if you don't believe me.) One of the important jobs of the neck is to provide flexibility to the body. Flexibility is also very important to consider in your investment body.

One element of flexibility in investing is liquidity—investments that you can convert to cash easily in an emergency. Most investors need to have some liquidity in their portfolios, if for no other reason than to take advantage of investment opportunities in the market. Having some liquidity means you only need to make one decision: what to buy. If you have to make two decisions—what to sell to provide the cash to then fund the purchase—the chances of that purchase happening will drop considerably. That may cause a pain in your neck that you would have preferred to avoid.

ALWAYS BUY ON SALE

The market, whether it's the market for stocks, bonds, real estate, or alternative types of investments, usually gives you opportunities to buy on sale. The most important factor to consider before you buy is the "why." How does the investment you intend to buy fit into your overall portfolio? Do you need to add some real estate exposure to your portfolio to get to your target mix of real estate? Do you need to find some stocks in the financial sector of the market to round out the diversification by economic sector in your portfolio? Whatever the reason, it is important to *have* a reason and not let emotions or the media drive the decision.

Once you have decided why you need the investment, evaluate the price. It is a good idea to put together a shopping list of items that you should add to your portfolio when the price and the time are right. Do your homework. Evaluate prices and valuations and be patient. As I said earlier, the market usually gives you an opportunity to buy on sale. I suggest setting a target price for the investment that is on your list and wait for the market to come to you. This usually allows you to buy the asset at a better price and valuation than you would get simply diving in at the prevailing price. If you do not know what I am talking about here, then you should hire an advisor to manage your portfolio (see Chapter 15).

TACTICAL ADJUSTMENTS TO YOUR PORTFOLIO

The flexibility factor also comes into play when we consider "tactical tilts" to the portfolio. A tactical tilt can be as simple as reducing small company stocks that may have become too expensive relative to large company stocks, or switching some of your assets between asset classes—such as between real estate and stocks or between stocks and bonds as the market presents opportunities. Keeping enough of the portfolio in easy-to-liquidate investments gives you the ability to take advantage of these opportunities.

LIQUIDITY VERSUS ILLIQUIDITY

In contrast, having too much liquidity—more than you would ever need and more than what you need to sleep well at night—can significantly detract from the return potential of your portfolio. Investors pay a significant penalty in terms of potentially lower returns in order to be liquid, yet most investors do not need to have their entire portfolios liquefiable on a moment's notice. The higher rate of return demanded for holding fewer liquid assets is referred to as the liquidity premium. The following chart (Figure 22) shows how much the liquidity premium costs investors heavily weighted in more liquid securities in different asset classes.

Figure 22   The Liquidity Premium

Performance of Publicly Traded Investments vs. Comparable Less Liquid Investments

	Liquid	Illiquid
Real Estate-Publicly Traded*	0.69**	
Real Estate-Private		1.09
Small-Cap Stocks	0.55	
Private Equity		1.02
Large-Cap Stocks	0.59	
Equity Hedge Funds		1.26

*These asset types are represented by the following indices: Public real estate—the National Association of Realtors All-REITs Index; Private real estate—NCRF Property Index; small-cap stocks—Russell 2000 Index; private equity—Cambridge U.S. Private Equity Index; large-cap stocks—S&P 500 Composite Index; and equity hedge—HFRI Equity Hedge Index. The Sharpe ratios cover the period from 1990 to 2004.
** The data in this table is the Sharpe Ratio. This ratio is defined in the Glossary section. The Sharpe ratios cover the period from 1990 to 2004.

Investors should think about how much illiquidity they can tolerate and what length of time they can have their investments locked up or illiquid. For example, an investor who decides he or she wants to go after higher returns in private equity investments should typically expect to not have access to that money for at least ten years.

Figure 23 illustrates typical "lock-up" periods for different asset types:

When thinking about the liquidity versus illiquidity decision, I suggest coming up with an actual percentage of the portfolio that you want to earmark for fewer liquid types of investments. Again, in most cases, this would be money you will not be able to tap into for several years.

Illiquidity, and even the potential for illiquidity, is an important issue for investors to understand. During the 2008–2009 bear market, certain invest-ments that were believed to be liquid turned out being illiquid as the market froze up and investors could not exit positions. Overestimating liquidity needs will generally give you some extra cushion of safety when considering what portion of your assets could be devoted to fewer liquid investments.

Once you have arrived at the percentage that can be devoted to illiquid investments, go back and review your asset allocation. Do you need more

Figure 23   Typical Lock-Up Periods for Different Investment Types

Type of Investment	Lock-Up Period
Hedge Funds	0 – 3 years
Private Equity	8 - 12 years
Private Real Estate	1 – 5 years
Exchange Funds	3 – 5 years
Timber	10 - 15 years
Commodity Funds	6 months – 2 years

Source: Author Analysis

exposure to real estate or to equities? That is important to know when deciding where you want to invest your fewer liquid investments.

STAY DISCIPLINED

As I mentioned earlier, one of the most challenging aspects of staying healthy in body and in investing is maintaining discipline. It is important to remember to stick to your game plan when things are not working right and not lose your focus when everything is going well.

A key element of investing over time is rebalancing. This means re-allocating your portfolio as the market gives you opportunities to scale back in one asset class and add to another in your portfolio. I have taken this concept a step further and dubbed it "averaging in, rebalancing out."

Averaging in, rebalancing out is essentially this: If you are below the target level for stocks in your portfolio, you can average in over a preset period of time to get to the target level. If you are above the target level of stocks in your portfolio, you can rebalance out to get back to your target.

Let's take the example of investors who missed the last two years of stock market recovery by having excess levels of cash in their portfolios. These investors want to get back into the market but worry about getting back in just before a market correction. Averaging in helps these investors step back into the market at different points in time, and likely at different price points.

What is the appropriate timeframe for averaging in? Investors can discover it by analyzing some hypothetical scenarios. For example, an investor with $1 million to put into the market might be thinking about averaging in over six months. How would this investor feel if the market were to gain 25 percent tomorrow and he or she missed an opportunity to make $250,000 by averaging in? On the flipside, if this same investor put the entire amount in the market today, and the market fell 25 percent the next day, how would he or she feel about losing $250,000 by not averaging in? This process can help investors find the right timeframe to balance opportunity and potential loss.

Rebalancing out is simply a way to reduce risk by cutting back exposure to assets that have run up in price and now represent a larger portion of the portfolio than what was targeted. There are a couple of ways to approach this. One is to rebalance periodically regardless of what the market has done. A better one is to set rebalancing rules that trigger a rebalancing when your actual allocation has drifted more than 5 or 10 percentage points away from your target. Either approach can help mitigate risk in the portfolio and provide discipline around your investment strategy. Remember to consider potential tax consequences and transactions costs before implementing this strategy.

Healthy Investment Tips

1. The degree of portfolio flexibility you want and need in the form of liquidity can have a significant impact on the return of your overall portfolio. It is a decision you should make consciously and not by default.

2. Develop a shopping list of investments you need to add to your portfolio and then strive to buy them on sale.

3. Using the averaging in, rebalancing out methods are an effective way to manage risk in your portfolio.

4. Develop an illiquidity target percentage for your portfolio, and then let your required asset allocation be a guide in directing you to the right types of less liquid investments.

10

The Heart: Keep Your Portfolio Pumping!

Heart: *The organ that pumps blood received from the veins into the arteries, thereby maintaining the flow of blood throughout the entire circulatory system*

The heart is crucial to life by pumping blood into every area of the body. In the investment world, the heart of an investment portfolio is often referred to as the core. The core of the portfolio provides an investor a source of reasonable growth as well as reasonable income. The investor can then build around that core and tilt investments to achieve either higher growth potential or higher income.

The sustaining part of the portfolio often comes from the generation of dividends and income over time. A sound portfolio provides a diversified stream of income and dividends, and a growing source of both if structured appropriately.

AN APPLE A DAY KEEPS THE DOCTOR AWAY

An apple fills you up and satisfies your hunger. It also has important vitamins that are good for your body. Dividend-paying stocks are like an apple; they can satisfy some of your income needs, but they can also provide growth opportunities in the form of rising income and appreciation of principal. Let's explore in more detail how dividend-paying stocks can be the apple that keeps the doctor away *and* an important cornerstone of your portfolio.

First, dividend-paying stocks pay out a portion of their earnings—typically, every quarter—to investors who hold the stock. These dividends can be used as a form of income to reinvest in the same stock or to purchase other investments. Dividends are like the blood pumped by the heart. Quality companies can provide a steady and consistent stream of dividends to the investor, giving the investor income to use, as needed.

Second, dividends force companies to think about shareholders and to consider a policy for regularly returning a portion of earnings to them. This acts as a form of discipline around the use of cash for the company that may be evaluating the payback of earnings versus the reinvestment of cash back into the company and the relative merits of each.

Third, dividends can dampen portfolio volatility. Companies that pay regular dividends are often more established companies and this, in and of itself, can reduce volatility. The dividend itself can act as a cushion in times of market turmoil in that it can preserve some investor wealth and help limit selling in a down market.

A fourth reason that dividends are important is that they can act as a significant income diversifier to other sources of investment income. Other income can often come from bonds, cash investments, and real estate. The income returns from these investments are often impacted by the interest rates in the economy, whereas stock dividends are less directly correlated to interest rates. In addition, as of this writing, the income on qualified stock dividends are taxed at a lower rate than income from many types of bonds and other income-like investments, providing the investor with another potential advantage.

The fifth and final reason that dividends are important is that they typically grow over time. Companies that are doing well generally increase their dividends to their investors on a regular basis. If a company that issues a bond is doing well, it will not say, "Gee, we are doing really well! Perhaps, we should pay our bond holders a higher interest rate." Sorry, that does not happen.

The following table (Figure 24) illustrates the impact of the dual forces of a lower tax rate and growing dividends on the after-tax income flow of dividend-paying stocks. In this particular example, the cumulative dividends from the common stock over the ten-year period equal 97 percent of the pre-tax income of the bond. The after-tax results are even more impressive in that the

Figure 24   A Lower Tax Rate on Dividends Could mean Higher After-Tax Income

	Stock	Dividend*	15% Tax-Rate After-Tax Dividend	Bond	Bond Interest	25% Tax-Rate After-Tax Interest
Starting Point	$100.00	$2.50	$2.12	$100.00	$4.75	$3.09
Year 2		2.83	2.40		4.75	3.09
Year 3		3.19	2.71		4.75	3.09
Year 4		3.61	3.07		4.75	3.09
Year 5		4.08	3.46		4.75	3.09
Year 6		4.61	3.92		4.75	3.09
Year 7		5.20	4.42		4.75	3.09
Year 8		5.88	5.00		4.75	3.09
Year 9		6.65	5.65		4.75	3.09
Year 10		7.51	6.38		4.75	3.09
		$46.05	$39.14		$47.50	$30.88

* Assumes a 13% annual dividend growth rate. If you have a 10-year investment time frame, consider allocating a portion of your income-producing portfolio to dividend-paying, dividend-growing stocks.

cumulative after-tax dividends from the stock represent 127 percent of the after-tax income from the bond.

If you want to look at it another way, take a look at selected companies listed in Figure 25 that demonstrated an ability to grow dividends over time. This table shows the yield on purchase price of each of these stocks at different points in time. This is a powerful illustration of just how big of a factor growing dividends can be, and why you should consider them for a portion of your portfolio.

There are some fantastic stories of dividend growth with some of the companies on this list. Take, for example, McDonald's. The yield on the twenty-year-ago purchase price of McDonald's is 33.5 percent. In other words, had you bought the stock twenty years ago and held it, the dividend yield today (based on your purchase price of twenty years ago) would be 33.5 percent— amazing!

This shows the potential income growth in investing in stocks that regularly increase their dividends over time. Even a number of companies on this list that have exhibited more modest dividend growth have fabulous yield-to-original purchase prices. Look at companies like Johnson & Johnson at 25.4 percent or Procter & Gamble at 19.3 percent—still impressive growers of income paid back to shareholders.

At the time of this book revision, our country may be embarking on significant changes in tax policy and tax rates that may complicate the analysis of dividends. There is the possibility that the 15 percent tax on dividends will be impacted in two ways: through higher tax rates for dividends and through an extra dividend tax for certain high-income investors in order to help pay for government spending and deficit reduction.

HEARTFELT FEELINGS

Our hearts are often referred to as the centers of our personalities, emotions, and feelings. The heart of your portfolio can also be your guide to connecting your feelings to your investment plan. So, when do you bring these elements into your investment plan?

The investment plan, in most cases, should be constructed using primarily the brain. After you have done that, you can then bring in the heart to make

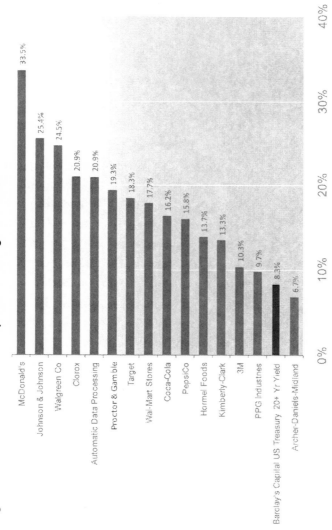

Figure 25 Selected Names of Companies Growing Dividends Over Time

This slide highlights a subset of the S&P Dividend Aristocrats index.

The chart plots the dividend yield (indicated annual dividend) relative to the company per share price 20 years ago (split adjusted). Also plotted on the chart is the Barclays Capital 20+ Year US Treasury yield as of 4/30/1991.

© 2011 Wells Fargo Bank, N.A. All rights reserved. Used with permission from Wells Fargo Bank, N. A.

sure it feels right for your personal situation. This can play out in a number of different ways. One that is common would be to overlay a socially responsible focus to your portfolio. This does not directly impact your overall plan from an asset allocation standpoint, but it may impact your plan in respect to the managers you use and the companies in which you invest. Connecting your investment portfolio to your heart can be an emotionally rewarding experience. If done correctly, it should not detract from your non-emotional results.

Let's explore socially responsible investing (SRI) in a little more detail. SRI can be as simple as screening companies based on your values, your heart, and your societal concerns. An SRI investor wants his or her investments to meet the criteria for a buyable investment that any other investment would meet.

Financial hurdles (e.g., earnings growth, revenue growth, valuation parameters, and sound positioning in their respective industry) are all important precursors to the SRI process. The difference is that SRI investors overlay additional criteria on the investment that may include, but are not limited to, such issues as environmental stewardship; religious values; employee rights; women's rights; diversity; human rights; animal use in product testing; tobacco, alcohol, and gambling; and defense and weapons production.

Figure 26 shows the growth in socially- and environmentally-screened portfolios over the past few years. From 1995 to 2007, there was a four-fold increase in investment assets screened on a variety of SRI factors.

SRI

People investing in SRI funds need to understand any potential risks they are taking by eliminating certain industries or sectors from their portfolio. It makes sense for SRI investors to evaluate the industry weightings in their portfolio versus the market to make sure they are comfortable with the relative weightings.

A rapidly growing area that is sometimes attributed to SRI is the area of alternative energy. This includes companies involved with wind power, solar energy, hydroelectric power, and ethanol production or technologies. Investment options for the typical investor just started to become more prevalent in this area in 2005. Many of the companies operating in this space are small and

Figure 26

Socially Responsible Investing in the US • 1995-2007

(In Billions)	1995	1997	1999	2001	2003	2005	2007
Social Screening	$162	$529	$1,497	$2,010	$2,143	$1,685	$2,098
Shareholder Advocacy	$473	$736	$922	$897	$448	$703	$739
Screening and Shareholder	N/A	($84)	($265)	($592)	($441)	($117)	($151)
Community Investing	$4	$4	$5	$8	$14	$20	$26
Total	**$639**	**$1,185**	**$2,159**	**$2,323**	**$2,164**	**$2,290**	**$2,711**

SOURCE: Social Investment Forum Foundation

NOTES: Social Screening includes socially and environmentally screened funds and separate account assets. Overlapping assets involved in Screening and Shareholder Advocacy are subtracted to avoid potential double-counting. Tracking Screening and Shareholder Advocacy together only began in 1997, so there is no datum for 1995. There are also potentially overlapping assets in the relatively small screened funds categories of Alternative Investments and Other Pooled Products; therefore these categories are also excluded from the SRI universe aggregated in this Report. See Chapter II for details.

Source: Social Investment Forum, 2007.

not currently profitable (as of this printing), and investors must be long-term focused, very patient, and keep their allocation limited if they want to be successful in this area.

One of the most promising areas of investing in alternative energy is in wind power. As you can see from Figure 27, wind power generation increased more than twenty-five-fold from 1996 to 2009. Wind power has advantages over many other energy sources because it is clean, renewable, can be generated in remote areas, and is cost competitive. Investing in companies at the forefront of wind power is currently difficult, with the best bets being established wind-turbine manufacturers and utilities.

Investors looking to invest in SRI can do so through one of three options:

1. **SRI mutual funds:** There are more than two hundred available in this category.
2. **ETFs:** There are numerous ETFs that invest with an SRI approach, but you must be careful in your analysis because several of these invest in a very narrow niche of the market. They may not be suitable for the amount of risk you want to take.
3. **SRI money manager:** Find someone who can customize a portfolio to your specific needs and concerns and apply SRI screens based on your criteria.

It has not been conclusively proven that socially responsible investing adds to portfolio returns or subtracts from them over time. As a result, most investors invest with these screens in mind not to get better performance, but to feel better about aligning their hearts with their investment strategy.

IMPACT INVESTING AND MICROFINANCE

A growing area of interest for many investors is what is now being called "impact investing." This goes beyond the search for companies that fulfill some SRI requirement. Impact investing is generally thought of as investing that can have a direct impact on social, environmental, or political changes that are important to the investor.

Microfinance is another area of growing interest for many wealthy investors and their families. This area of investing allows investors to directly

Figure 27   Cumulative Installed Wind Capacity

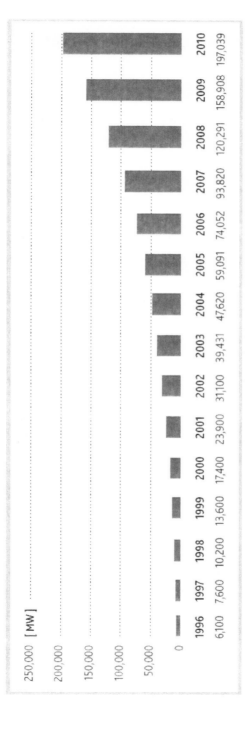

GLOBAL CUMULATIVE INSTALLED WIND CAPACITY 1996-2010

1996	1997	1998	1999	2000	2001	2002	2003	2004	2005	2006	2007	2008	2009	2010
6,100	7,600	10,200	13,600	17,400	23,900	31,100	39,431	47,620	59,091	74,052	93,820	120,291	158,908	197,039

Source: GWEC - Global Wind Energy Council, Global Wind Report 2010

invest in projects that they feel will have tangible and possibly more immediate benefits to the causes they are interested in supporting.

DANGERS TO THE HEART

Not enough exercise, poor eating habits, unhealthy lifestyle choices, and high
cholesterol are some key factors that negatively impact the heart. The cholesterol in investment portfolios is called "leverage." While poor eating habits
can seem enjoyable at the time, they eventually catch up to you. That does not
mean you cannot indulge in some of your favorite foods periodically; it just
needs to be done with a sense of reason. The same is true for leverage. Used
inappropriately, or in large portions, it can result in an arrhythmia in your
portfolio. On the flipside, used with the right measure, it can enhance your
returns.

In a bull market, leverage can make an investor look really smart. Leverage
in a bear market, or correction, can make you look stupid—or worse. The key
is to think about how it changes your risk profile and whether or not you and
your portfolio can handle the added risk.

In the bull market of the 1990s, the use of leverage applied to a concentrated stock position was a popular way for an investor to develop a so-called
completion portfolio. That completion portfolio was essentially a portfolio of
stocks funded with a loan that was backed by the value of the concentrated
stock. If the concentrated stock goes up in value, and the stocks that you buy
from the proceeds of the loan go up in value, you can look really smart—as
long as the gains exceed the interest you pay on the loan. However, if the concentrated stock goes down in value, and/or the stocks you buy go down in
value, you can experience a portfolio loss greater than if you had done nothing
at all. Oh, and you would still have to pay back the loan *and* the interest.

Professional investors can lever up portfolios and, in many cases, manage
risks effectively by arbitraging interest-rate differentials between countries or
across different maturities. This can take the form of borrowing in Japanese
yen at 1 percent and investing in New Zealand bonds at 7 percent. Or it could
mean borrowing at 1 percent and buying stock while hoping for the price of
the stock to rise. Often, professional investors have an added advantage in
being able to borrow money at lower rates than individual investors.

The use of leverage by professional investors can still be very dangerous, and you should understand the amount of leverage that they are taking on your behalf. Many investment vehicles that use leverage report this data to shareholders on a periodic basis. If that is not the case with your investments, I suggest you ask for that information and make your own determination if you are comfortable with that degree of leverage. Value at Risk (VaR) is a common way to analyze the risk of a portfolio (including the leverage factor). Refer to the glossary at the back of the book for a definition of VaR, or better yet, ask the manager of your portfolio, or any investment in which you may place money, to provide you with a more detailed explanation. Essentially, it is a stress test of the downside risk in your portfolio, or in a specific investment, and it gives you a sense of whether or not you could the handle the risk when it rears its ugly head.

LIFESTYLES OF THE ACTIVE OR PASSIVE

We all know that living an active lifestyle versus a passive lifestyle has implications for our hearts and our overall health. What about investing? Some financial advisors make a big deal about whether investors should invest actively or passively. The question that starts the debate goes like this: "Do you think active investing is superior to passive investing (or vice versa)?" Those in either camp can debate the answer to this question quite passionately. They can make arguments about cost differences, the degree to which active managers beat an index or not, whether the market is efficient or inefficient, and so forth.

From a practical standpoint, the debate about active versus passive is inconsequential to most investors because there are a lot more meaningful things to worry about—for example, how you should structure your portfolio for the highest probability of meeting your goals. The primary debate of active versus passive investing revolves around indexing, or passive investing. The indexing issue is focused on whether or not an active manager can beat the returns of an index consistently over time. In other words, would you be better off just buying an investment vehicle that mimics the index? Let's start to answer this by taking a look at some of the advantages and disadvantages of each approach.

I believe that the primary advantage indexing has over active investing is that it is relatively inexpensive. An investor should be able to save between 0.5 to 1 percent per year in management fees by indexing rather than using an active management approach. The reason for this cost difference is that there is little to no research, analysis, and ongoing monitoring of investments taking place in an index fund; that is why it is referred to as passive. The active functions of constantly trying to find the best opportunities in the market cost investors money.

A key question relative to the cost debate is concentrated on the asset class you are looking at and the degree to which managers have been able to add enough value to cover the added costs of active management. Figure 28 shows how much value is typically added between the median manager and a manager at the bottom of the top quartile. From this data, you can see that active management in the alternative asset categories has the potential to add significant value. The performance differences between top manager and median manager can even be quite large in this area.

There also continues to be significant opportunities for active management to add value in international and domestic equity markets. There appears to be less advantage in the highest quality fixed income space for active management to add value from a pure performance perspective. However, active management in areas such as high-yield, tax-exempt international and emerging fixed income markets may have significant active management benefits. Additionally, as the fixed income markets have changed over time, the need for active credit research to reduce or control risk is an important consideration in this debate.

Let's switch gears and look at the two primary disadvantages of passive investing. The first one relates to what I call "buying high." Most indices that passive investors use to invest in are market capitalization-weighted. What this means is that companies that have more market value have the greatest weight in the index. The market value is calculated by multiplying the share price by the number of shares that are outstanding.

This market capitalization bias results in you buying more of what is expensive and/or large in the index and less of what is inexpensive and/or small in the index. For example, in 1999, the S&P 500 had more than 40 percent of its total value and index weighting invested in the technology sector.

Figure 28 Difference in Active Return by Asset Class

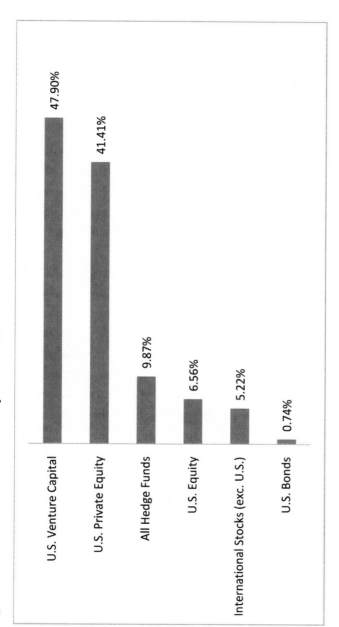

Data is difference in manager performance between bottom of 1st quartile and bottom of 2nd quartile.

1st Quartile vs. 2nd Quartile

January 1990 - December 2010

Source: Rogerscasey, July 2011

The reason for the high weighting is the dramatic rise of technology stocks in the mid- to late 1990s. On a relative basis, they went up significantly more than stocks in most other industries.

Buying that index in 1999 would have not only resulted in you buying those technology stocks at unsustainably high prices, but it also would have given you a disproportionate weighting to the technology industry. In contrast, buying the S&P 500 in 1999 would have given you only a 5 percent weighting to energy stocks, which were ridiculously cheap at that time.

The second disadvantage to indexing is what I just discussed: sector weightings. Many investors think that index funds are well-diversified across both companies and industries. In many respects, this is true. However, from a relative weighting perspective, you could be very much over- or underweight in key industry sectors that are underappreciated in the market, but have excellent forward opportunities.

So, what are some other advantages of passive investing? In addition to cost, this way of investing is generally pretty easy. There are numerous options in the mutual fund and ETF world that can give an investor exposure to different types of investments, different-sized companies, different industry sectors, and even different investment-style categories. These different parts of the market have a wide array of indices that the investment industry has created index products around so investors can invest in them. Many of these products can be used by investors as temporary investments meant to get exposure to different parts of the market. Investors with money to invest can utilize these passive strategies to get market exposure while they research potential active managers in those asset categories.

One way that active and passive investing can be used in combination for the benefit of investors is when you are looking to include some managers in your portfolio who have broad latitude to invest beyond the benchmark. In other words, these managers are less restricted by staying close to the benchmark in their search for opportunities. These managers tend to have "high tracking error," and we will discuss this concept later in the book. For now, it may make sense to consider combining active managers with broad latitude to invest beyond the benchmark with passive investments to reduce the overall risk of underperforming the market. Doing so will give you a chance to invest in active managers who can use their skills to potentially benefit your overall results.

It is my belief that active managers and passive investing can coexist peacefully in most investors' portfolios. In other words, there can be a role for each within the context of a portfolio and the day-to-day management of that portfolio.

PASSIVE INVESTING SUMMARIZED

1. Passive-only investing has the disadvantage of obtaining more of what is expensive and less of what is inexpensive.

2. Passive investing can lead to being extremely overweight or underweight in industry sectors relative to their importance in the economy and future prospects.

3. Passive investing can lower your overall investment costs.

4. Passive investing can give you quick exposure to different parts of the market.

5. Passive investing options are widely available for most investors.

6. Passive investing can be used as a portfolio management tool while looking for active managers or implementing a tax-loss harvesting strategy.

7. Passive investing does not let you avoid bad companies. You buy them all—the good, the bad, and the ugly.

ACTIVE INVESTING SUMMARIZED

1. Active management can offer investors a chance to pursue returns above an index return.

2. Active management can offer investors a portfolio that has less risk than an index and can potentially protect principal better in a down market.

3. Active management runs the risk of not being able to match the returns of an index if the manager is not successful in the investment approach.

4. Active management allows for the customization of a portfolio to more accurately represent the goals and wishes of the investor.

5. Active management allows for the potential to manage the timing of tax impact for the investor (if done in a separate account format).

Healthy Investment Tips

1. Structure your portfolio with a core that can provide a steady flow of dividends and income that will satisfy your spending needs.
2. Investing with your heart can also mean applying some SRI principles. This can also be a means to help you be more engaged in thinking about your investment portfolio, especially if you are not wired to normally think about it.
3. When investing with your heart, it is important to not omit key sectors of the economy or make concentrated bets.
4. You should seek to understand the amount of leverage that is being used in your portfolio and whether you are comfortable with the added risk that this brings to your portfolio's health.
5. There is a role for both active and passive investment approaches within most investors' portfolios.

11

The Lungs and Kidneys: Breathing New Life into Your Portfolio

Lung: *Occupies the chest cavity together with the heart; functions to remove carbon dioxide from the blood and provide it with oxygen*

Kidney: *Functions to maintain proper water and electrolytic balance; filters waste within the body*

Let's start this chapter by focusing on the themes related to breathing new life into your portfolio and eliminating the waste. This is probably good advice for lots of areas of your life, not just investing. It is important to keep feeding oxygen, or ideas, into your portfolio. The new ideas help to keep the portfolio from getting stale and the investor from getting bored. Portfolios need constant monitoring, and the best way to keep on top of it is to be thinking of new ideas to improve or enhance your portfolio.

It is also important to periodically cleanse your portfolio, not just of bad investments that did not turn out as expected, but to realize important tax benefits. Most investors do not think about the management of taxes as a year-round process in their portfolios. Taking advantage of year-round tax-loss harvesting can be a great way to improve your after-tax portfolio return. (This should be very important to taxable investors.)

RUNNING AN EFFICIENT BODY: INVESTING FOR TAX EFFICIENCY

Most of us have the privilege of paying taxes. In some cases, we may be paying taxes in the 35 percent federal bracket and in a state bracket that ranges from 5 to 10 percent. This means that, for some of us, taxes consume more than 45 percent of our taxable income. As a result, if we can invest with an eye toward lowering the impact that taxes have on our portfolios, we could potentially add a lot of value.

In this chapter, I cover several key elements of managing your portfolio with tax efficiency in mind. I cover the difference between tax-deferred and tax-exempt; what types of assets to hold in your taxable accounts and what types to hold in your tax-deferred accounts; tax-loss harvesting strategies; and alternative minimum tax (AMT).

A survey of investors completed in early 2011 by the Spectrum Group indicated that tax increases and what the tax increases would mean for investment strategy are top concerns of investors (see Figure 29).

TAX-DEFERRED VERSUS TAX-EXEMPT

"Tax-deferred" means you still owe the tax, just not now. This is true for investments in IRA accounts, 401(k) plans, annuities, and other tax-qualified investment vehicles. You can generally shelter the income or gains on investments within these vehicles until you take the money out. Once you take it out, it will be taxed at your ordinary income tax rate. That still gives you a big advantage, however, allowing those assets to grow without the need to immediately pay taxes on them. It also allows you to take gains within those accounts if you believe something is highly valued or over-valued without the worry about what the tax bill will be. But eventually the tax will need to be paid, usually when you start withdrawing from these accounts.

"Tax-exempt" means you do not owe the tax now, and you do not owe the tax in the future. You are not building up some future tax liability; you simply do not pay taxes now or in the future on tax-exempt investments. The most common example of a tax-exempt investment is a municipal bond—also referred to as tax-exempt bond. Interest from municipal bonds is exempt from federal taxes and, in some cases, exempt from state taxes as well.

Figure 29   Portfolio Strategy Concerns

	Investor %
Increase in taxes	71%
Tax increases means a change in investment strategy	48%
Sale of assets to maintain current standard of living	15%
Impact of recession means delaying retirement	10%
Impact of recession could result in an eventual lower standard of living	8%

Wondering what to hold in your taxable accounts and what to hold in your tax-deferred accounts? This decision is dependent on your ordinary income tax rates and capital gains tax rates. As of this writing, we have very favorable capital gains tax rates and equally favorable tax rates on stock dividends. In other words, there is currently a big differential between ordinary tax rates on bond interest and capital gains tax rates on the long-term gains on stocks (15 percent maximum capital gains tax rate). In that environment, it may make sense to keep some stocks in taxable accounts and pay the relatively low capital gains rates. High-income investments—such as corporate bonds or real estate investment trusts—not subject to the lower dividend tax rates may make sense in tax-deferred accounts like an IRA.

Investment styles that have heavy turnover and a high proportion of short-term gains taxed at ordinary rates may be best positioned in tax-deferred accounts. Generally, small company stock funds and managers have much higher turnover and potential tax impact than large company funds and managers. In many cases, hedge funds, managed futures investments, and commodities investing also generate significant short-term gains that can benefit from tax-deferred accounts.

A counterargument to the bonds going in taxable accounts can be in environments where municipal bonds, or tax-exempt bonds, are very attractive for your tax bracket and relative to taxable bonds available in the market. In those situations, it may make sense to create a tax-exempt bond portfolio and put them in a taxable account to realize the benefit of the tax exemption. It should go without saying—but I have seen it happen—that you should generally not put tax-exempt bonds in a tax-deferred account.

TAX-LOSS HARVESTING STRATEGIES

Often, investors start thinking about tax-loss harvesting close to the end of the year. They, or their accountants, tally up the gains they have realized to date and decide that some losses should be taken to reduce the tax impact on the gains. By waiting until the end of the year, however, investors potentially miss out on huge opportunities presented throughout the course of the year.

If you do not have the time to engage in active tax-loss harvesting, hire a professional investment advisor who includes tax-loss harvesting as a part of his or her process. By being smart about tax-loss harvesting strategies, a good advisor may be able to cover his or her fees in most years from what he or she save you in taxes alone.

The following is a list of some common tax-loss harvesting strategies you may be able to employ in your portfolio.

Selected Tax-Loss Harvesting Strategies

1. Take a loss on any individual investment where the current price has dropped by more than 10 percent from the original cost.

    a. *Sell the stock and buy an ETF in the same industry sector.* Buying the ETF in the same industry allows you to keep industry exposure while harvesting the loss. This allows you to potentially recover some of the loss if the sector recovers while you are out of the stock. After thirty-one days, sell the ETF, and buy back the stock if you still want to own it.

b. *Sell the stock and buy a different stock in the same industry.* After thirty-one days, you can buy back the original stock and not be worried about the wash sale rule.

c. *Double-up.* In this strategy, you buy additional shares in the same stock that you have the loss. After thirty-one days, you can sell your original shares to realize the loss. The advantage of this strategy is if the specific stock in which you have a loss makes a quick recovery, you will not be out of the game. The potential disadvantages are that it requires more funds to buy the extra stock, and it subjects you to more risk to that same stock during the thirty-one days that you have double the position in place.

2. Take losses on individual bonds. If you experience a rapid increase in interest rates and you own bonds, you probably have a loss. How? The value of the bonds you own goes down if interest rates go up because an investor will pay you less for a bond that has an interest rate below that of the current market. You can take advantage of that loss by selling the bond at a loss and realizing that loss for tax purposes.

3. Bond fund investors can also take losses if the current value of the fund is less than your purchase price. You could sell the fund and buy a different bond fund to keep bond exposure in your portfolio, yet realize the tax loss. Investors need to be careful to check that they do not have redemption fees, back-end loads, or other charges that would make this strategy impractical.

ALTERNATIVE MINIMUM TAX

The main thing an investor must watch out for with AMT is private activity municipal bonds. These bonds are tied to a specific project and are often subject to AMT tax, which could result in a higher tax bill. The other thing to monitor with AMT is the amount of stock options you exercise in any given year. This can be a significant contributor to AMT if you work for a company that issues stock options as part of your compensation. A certain level of stock option gains will often trigger AMT issues. It is best to work with a tax professional to understand how these factors can impact your after-tax investment returns.

REBALANCING STRATEGIES

Rebalancing also enters the picture here. I have already discussed the importance of asset allocation and maintaining the right mix of investments in your portfolio. The only way to maintain that mix is to periodically rebalance the portfolio. To follow our anatomy theme for this section, this helps to keep you from becoming out of breath (lungs—get it?).

Many investors will let the mix of their investments drift. Over time, as assets perform differently, percentage allocations will also change. Figure 30 shows how dangerous it can be to your wealth to allow that to happen.

In scenario one, many investors likely convinced themselves that they could live with a 63 percent weighting to stocks even though their target had originally been 50 percent. The risk profile of a 63 percent stock portfolio is higher than a 50 percent stock portfolio, as indicated in the portfolio risk column. These investors had experienced a tremendously positive bull market in stocks that convinced them they could handle the additional risk, especially since they experienced very few downdrafts along the way.

The subsequent drop in the market resulted in an additional loss of $46,800 in a $1 million portfolio. This was just the loss due to not rebalancing stocks back to their target mix. This does not include the return difference the investor would have enjoyed having a higher percentage in bonds during the stock market pullback.

In scenario two, the investor with a 50/50 mix at the beginning of a bear market saw his mix of stocks drop from 50 percent to 32 percent as the stock market dropped. This situation would have been a great opportunity to rebalance to the 50 percent weighting by buying stocks on sale. Emotionally, such rebalancing is very difficult to do, which is why the process should be as mechanical or rules-driven as possible. Rebalancing would have positioned the investor for a potential increased return of $90,000 in the market rebound over the next two years.

Figure 30   Two Rebalancing Examples

Scenario 1: Investor Does Not Rebalance, then Stocks Plummet

Portfolio Allocation

Date	Stocks*	Bonds*	Portfolio Risk*
January 1, 2003	50%	50%	8.56%
December 31, 2006	63%	37%	10.18%

Over the next two years, the S&P 500 stock index drops 36%. Investor loses more than he would have if his portfolio had been rebalanced regularly.

Scenario 2: Investor Does Not Rebalance, then Stocks Soar

Portfolio Allocation

Date	Stocks*	Bonds*	Portfolio Risk*
November 1, 2007	50%	50%	6.38%
February 28, 2009	32%	68%	4.91%

Over the next fourteen months, the S&P 500 stock index climbs 65%. Investor profits less than he would have if his portfolio had been rebalanced regularly.

* Stocks are represented by the S&P 500 Index. Bonds are represented by the Barclays Capital U.S. Aggregate Bond Index (formerly known as Lehman Brothers U.S. Aggregate Bond Index). The portfolio risk is the standard deviation of the portfolio.

Figure 31 shows an example of the power of rebalancing. In this example, quarterly rebalancing added 8.7 percent of performance over a three-year period versus a buy and hold approach.

There are many schools of thought on the correct way for investors to rebalance their portfolios. Basically, there are two approaches you can take. The most common approach is to rebalance on a set time schedule—typically, either quarterly or annually. The other method is to rebalance when any of the asset classes (stocks, bonds, real estate, alternatives, etc.) are more than 5 or 10 percent away from their targets.

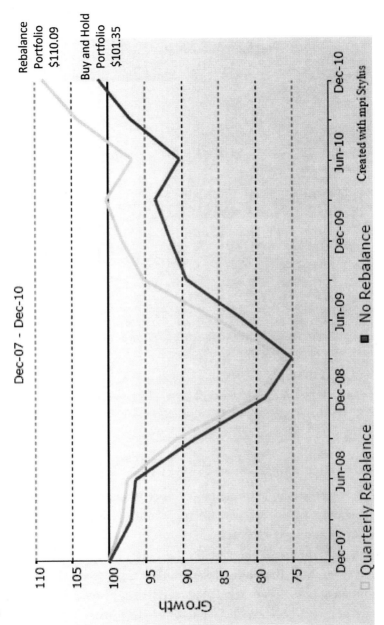

Figure 31 Cumulative Performance

Dec-07 - Dec-10

Source: Wells Fargo Wealth Management, Balanced Portfolio allocations from published Asset Allocation Strategy Reports, Dec. 2007 – Dec. 2010. Indicies represent asset classes.

Numerous studies have looked into the different approaches to rebalancing and have attempted to determine which is best. In case you are interested, I have included a one-page synopsis of several of the studies in Appendix V. My view is that rebalancing is most effective when asset groups are out of balance by at least 5 percent. At that point, you should consider rebalancing. When the groups are out of balance by 10 percent, you should at least rebalance to within 5 percent of your target.

Whether you go all the way back to your strategic mix can be influenced by the cost of rebalancing—taxes and trading costs—and the degree to which valuation extremes exist between asset groups in your portfolio. In other words, if you are overweight on your real estate target by 10 percent, and real estate is very expensive in the market, I would suggest that you rebalance all the way to your target. Of course, consideration to taxes and the cost of the rebalancing transaction need to be considered.

In addition to rebalancing between asset classes, it is also important to rebalance within asset classes and within economic sectors. For example, you may be in an environment in which value stocks have outperformed growth stocks for a long time. As a result, your portfolio may be significantly overweight in regards to value. The appropriate action may be to consider rebalancing by trimming back some of your value holdings and adding to your growth holdings.

In the case of economic sectors, we regularly go through periods of time in the market where one or two economic sectors will dominate, and the performance of those sectors will far exceed the performance of the other sectors in your portfolio. This will likely result in your portfolio having larger or smaller weightings in economic sectors of the market than what you would like to see or what would constitute as a well-balanced portfolio. Rebalancing by trimming back those heavily weighted sectors will reduce the risk in your portfolio and likely result in a better long-term experience.

Healthy Investment Tips

1. Tax-efficient investing and harvesting losses can contribute significantly to your after-tax investment returns.
2. Tax-deferred investments are not the same as tax-exempt investments, and you should consider how to best use these in your overall portfolio.

3. There may be advantages to place certain types of investments in tax-deferred accounts and other types in taxable accounts to take advantage of the tax characteristics of different investment types.

4. Rebalancing your strategic asset allocation mix, as needed, is an important tactic to keep your portfolio healthy over time.

12

The Arms and Legs: Portfolio Construction and Investment Vehicles

Leg: A limb or appendage of the body; used for locomotion or support

Arm: A limb or appendage of the body; connects the hand and wrist to the shoulder

This is where the rubber meets the road in your portfolio. Many folks in the investment world refer to this as "portfolio construction." It is not coincidental that I have this as the second to the last item in the investment process flow chart shown below.

Portfolio construction is very important to your overall investment plan, but it should not be dealt with until you have created a thorough investment plan, incorporating all of the other anatomical elements. There is a tendency for the investor to want to take action (arms and legs), but patience is critical here. Figure 32 illustrates the key steps to a rational investment process and where portfolio construction fits into the picture:

Many investors—and sometimes their advisors—want to jump right to portfolio construction. At the risk of redundancy, I highly encourage you to go through the whole process (and in order).

Figure 32   Investment Process Flow Chart

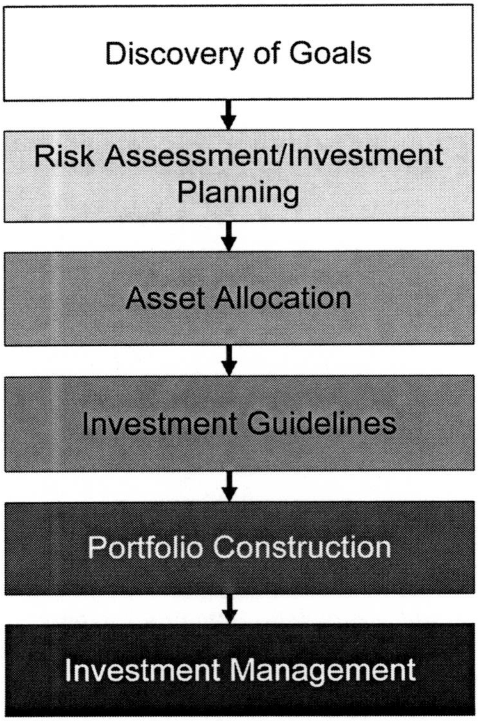

```
┌─────────────────────────────────┐
│       Discovery of Goals        │
└─────────────────────────────────┘
                 │
                 ▼
┌─────────────────────────────────┐
│   Risk Assessment/Investment    │
│            Planning             │
└─────────────────────────────────┘
                 │
                 ▼
┌─────────────────────────────────┐
│        Asset Allocation         │
└─────────────────────────────────┘
                 │
                 ▼
┌─────────────────────────────────┐
│      Investment Guidelines      │
└─────────────────────────────────┘
                 │
                 ▼
┌─────────────────────────────────┐
│      Portfolio Construction     │
└─────────────────────────────────┘
                 │
                 ▼
┌─────────────────────────────────┐
│      Investment Management      │
└─────────────────────────────────┘
```

Source: Author Analysis

THE PROCESS OF SELECTING A MANAGER FOR CONSIDERATION

The traditional method of selecting an investment manager often begins with reviewing the historical return profile. In my view, past performance alone is not a reliable predictor of future results. I believe that investment firms with sound investment strategies, outstanding human capital, and consistent investment processes increase the probability of a better outcome for investors.

A sound manager evaluation process is designed to separate skill from luck, comprehend the risks a manager assumes, and determine whether his or her strategy is sustainable in the long run. The entire process is aimed at identifying a group of investment managers who we believe have the greatest potential to meet or exceed expectations (while taking the appropriate level of risk). In my opinion, improving your odds of success around manager selection depends on five key factors: a proven framework to evaluate ideas; experienced analysts who know what to look for; access to a broad range of investment opportunities; objectivity; and understanding of the performance cycle of great money managers.

SELECTING THE RIGHT INVESTMENTS FOR YOUR PORTFOLIO

Portfolio construction is where you actually get to start choosing the investments that will make up your portfolio. Many considerations should go into portfolio construction, including the pros and cons of each type of investment vehicle you are considering for your portfolio. I address some of these considerations in Figure 33.

Figure 33   Portfolio Construction Considerations

Investment Vehicle	Pros	Cons
Individual Securities	• Know what you own • Control timing of gains	• Lots of monitoring required • Diversification can be difficult
Mutual Funds (Open End)	• Ease of purchase • Diversification • Professional Management	• No control over taxes • No assurance of market returns • Investment overlap potential • Additional fees • Potential purchase of tax liability
Separately-Managed Accounts	• Know what you own • Some customization • Professional management • Manager due diligence	• Large portfolio required • Several managers required to achieve style and class • Diversification
ETF's	• Ease of purchase • Control over taxes • Relatively low expense ratio • No built in tax liability	• Most have limited excess return potential
Closed-End Funds	• Ease of daily buy/sell • Higher return potential	• Use of leverage • Potentially high trading costs
Annuities	• Tax deferral • Death benefit	• High cost • Liquidity constraints

Source: Author Analysis

There are several key factors that influence which of these investment vehicles to use in your portfolio. Some of the key factors include: the size of your portfolio; the various costs associated with each vehicle; the ease of entry into the investment vehicle; and the degree to which you want to be actively involved in the last step in the investment process—investment management.

Investment management is the ongoing management and monitoring of your portfolio investments. This is the last step in the investment process, but a step that is ongoing. If you decide you want to own individual securities, this step of the process will involve a lot of time and energy. In order to get the diversification you need across industries, companies, size, and geography, you will probably need at least $250,000 for the stock portion of your portfolio to effectively utilize individual names.

If you want to use ETFs, the time commitment required to manage the portfolio will be less than with individual securities, but the ongoing expense ratios built into the ETFs may be higher. You also need to do some work on the front end to make sure you buy the right ETFs for the asset allocation needs of your portfolio. One significant area to explore with ETFs is concentration risk. Many ETFs have been created focused on only one sector of the market—one country, one style of investing, or one size of company. Some ETFs investing in narrow sectors may be highly concentrated in the one or two dominant companies in the industry and, as a result, their performance heavily depends on those one or two companies. This is not the diversification you may have expected, so look at the holdings and the weightings in each!

The analysis and ongoing management of a mutual fund portfolio or a separately managed account portfolio can be just as time-consuming and possibly more complex than managing an individual securities portfolio. In most cases, it will make sense for you to hire a professional advisor to get the most out of this experience.

CEFs are the second cousin to open-end mutual funds (OEFs). There are some benefits to CEFs—primarily their ease of trading—since they trade like a stock on the public exchanges. From a management perspective, the CEF manager has a fixed pool of investments to manage and does not need to worry about the flow of money into and out of the fund. The manager also has the ability to use leverage to potentially enhance returns and yields. This can create returns and yields that look appealing to individual investors but come with higher risks.

From time to time, investors can find appealing opportunities in CEFs that are trading at significant discounts to their net asset value (NAV). The fund could be trading below the NAV for a whole host of reasons. It could be simply that the fund style is out of favor and the fund is trading very thinly, which means little activity or interest from investors. In some cases, this allows an investor to buy assets at a discount. For example, you may be able to find a fund that trades for 85 or 90 cents on the dollar, which can be very appealing if the fund fits into your overall investment strategy.

Healthy Investment Tips

1. Don't start selecting investment vehicles for your portfolio until you have addressed the other steps of the investment process outlined in this chapter.
2. Understand the process of selecting managers and investment for consideration in your portfolio.
3. When selecting investing vehicles, make sure you understand the pros and cons of each, and how to best use them in your portfolio.
4. Investment management is the last step in the investment process, but requires ongoing involvement by the investor and/or advisor.

13

The Annual Physical: The Annual Portfolio Review

Physical: The diagnostic process that provides for an evaluation of your health

Most doctors recommend that people get an annual physical after a certain age. This serves as a way to identify problems before they develop or get out of control. If necessary, the annual physical can be the catalyst to adjustments in your life to head off problems before they become serious. The same benefits apply to an annual portfolio review.

Simply put, the annual portfolio review should include the following:

1. A review of any changes in your life that might impact your investment portfolio or investment plan in any way.

2. A review of your investment plan even if there has been no change since last review. It just makes sense to focus on your stated investment plan and be reminded of that plan before you start digging into the specifics of your portfolio.

3. A review of your asset allocation. Has it changed significantly due to the market or to withdrawals from your investments? Do you need to rebalance to your target asset allocation?

4. An evaluation of each asset class represented in your portfolio and an examination of whether or not they are performing as expected and fulfilling their role in the portfolio.

5. A review of your overall portfolio in relation to your stated goals and investment plan.

6. A decision as to when you will schedule the next annual portfolio review.

Here is a simple checklist to help in the annual review process. Ask yourself and your family members the following questions to determine if any changes need to be made to your investment plan:

1. What has changed in our lives? A new child, a new spouse, a new job, a new house, a second or third house, a change in health, etc?

2. Have these changes altered our priorities?

3. Have there been any changes in income? Is it higher or lower? Has the frequency of income changed?

4. Have there been any changes in expenses? Are they higher or lower?

5. Has there been any change in state of residence?

6. Has our tax bracket changed?

7. Have our goals changed?

8. Has there been a change in our risk tolerance? (This might have been prompted by various reasons, including changes in some of the above items.)

Once you have asked these questions, review your investment policy statement (which is written documentation of your investment plan) to see if anything needs to be changed or updated. If changes need to be made, make sure they are updated and then communicated to your advisor(s).

BLOOD PRESSURE: BOND MATH, BOND TYPES, AND ANALYSIS

There are two important numbers to consider when looking at your blood pressure reading. Admittedly, this may be a stretch as far as the analogy goes, but the same is true for bonds. The numbers for bonds are a little different—

the taxable yield and the taxable equivalent yield. Let me explain why these two numbers are important.

Most individual investors pay taxes. As a result, investors not only want to know the level of income they will receive before tax, they also want to know how much will be left after the taxes are paid. Bonds available to investors may be subject to different types of taxes. Some are subject to both state and federal taxes. Other bonds are subject to either just state taxes or just federal taxes. Last, but certainly not least, there are other bonds that are exempt from both state and federal taxes. The differences between types of bonds and their taxability are shown in Figure 34.

How do you evaluate whether a taxable bond or a tax-exempt bond is the best option for you? There are two main considerations: the credit quality and the taxable equivalent yield. Again, this is sort of like the blood pressure reading. The numbers of your blood pressure reflect the high- and low-pressure readings in your arteries. Generally speaking, when it comes to a bond, the higher the credit rating, the lower the yield.

The credit quality issue is relatively straightforward when evaluating U.S. Treasury, agency, and corporate bonds. U.S. Treasury bonds are backed by the

Figure 34   Bond Types and Taxability

Type of Bond	Exempt from Federal Tax	Exempt from State Tax
U.S. Government Bonds	No	Yes
U.S. Government Agency Bonds	No	Yes[*]
Corporate Bonds	No	No
Municipal Bonds (also referred to as "tax-exempt bonds)	Yes	Possibly[**]

[*]Certain government agency bonds issued by the FHLMC and FNMA are exempt from state taxes; others are typically not. See your tax advisor for more information.
[**]Municipal Bonds are generally state income tax-exempt if you hold bonds issued in the state which you claim residency for tax purposes.

Source: Author Analysis

full faith and credit of the U.S. government and are widely considered to be the highest quality bonds available to investors.

Agency bonds, or bonds issued by agencies of the federal government, are generally considered to have an implied guarantee by the government, but not a direct guarantee. The credit rating agencies usually assign their highest ratings to agency bonds (although, as of this writing, that may be changing).

Corporate bonds, or bonds issued by corporations, are usually followed and rated by the major rating agencies. Most corporate bonds of larger companies would be rated by both S&P and Moody's and assigned an alphabetical-style rating scheme. Figures 35 and 36 summarize the ratings of these two prominent rating agencies.

Figure 36 illustrates the default risk in lower-rated bonds. For example, after ten years, 69 percent of "Caa" bonds (Moody's lowest rating) defaulted during a study period from 1970 to 2006. Compare that to less than 0.6 of 1 percent of bonds rated "Aaa" that defaulted over a ten-year period during the same study.

It is important to note that just because a bond or a bond-like investment has a high credit rating—even an AAA rating—this is not a guarantee that you will not lose money. Many investment firms have put together products backed by AAA- or AA-rated bonds that carry many other risks, including repayment risks and leverage risks. In some cases, these risks can be more substantial than the credit risk of the bond. The bottom line here is to make sure you know what you own. If you don't have the systems and resources to evaluate all the risks of bond investing, you should consider hiring a professional.

For an example of risks that can come from high-rated bonds, the financial crisis of 2008 and early 2009 provides a good case study. Many mortgage-backed securities filled with or heavily weighted to subprime mortgages or interest-only-type mortgages experienced severe price deterioration, causing significant loses to investors. In some cases, these securities carried the highest ratings from the rating agencies. This, again, provides an example that high ratings are not an assurance that losses will not occur.

In the municipal bond world, many municipalities are rated by the rating agencies, but some are not. This is especially true for smaller municipalities

Figure 35 S&P's Cumulative Average Default Rates

Cumulative Average Default Rates, 1981 - 2005 (%)															
						--Time Horizon (Year)--									
Rating	**1**	**2**	**3**	**4**	**5**	**6**	**7**	**8**	**9**	**10**	**11**	**12**	**13**	**14**	**15**
AAA	0.00	0.00	0.03	0.06	0.10	0.17	0.24	0.36	0.40	0.44	0.44	0.44	0.44	0.51	0.58
AA	0.01	0.04	0.09	0.19	0.29	0.40	0.52	0.62	0.71	0.81	0.91	1.01	1.12	1.22	1.28
A	0.04	0.12	0.23	0.38	0.59	0.81	1.06	1.29	1.55	1.83	2.06	2.26	2.44	2.60	2.85
BBB	0.27	0.76	1.32	2.06	2.83	3.56	4.15	4.76	5.27	5.82	6.37	6.80	7.29	7.77	8.32
BB	1.12	3.33	5.96	8.45	10.65	12.77	14.45	15.90	17.26	18.29	19.25	19.97	20.62	21.05	21.58
B	5.38	11.80	17.14	21.24	24.16	26.45	28.37	29.91	31.15	32.38	33.48	34.44	35.44	36.34	37.18
CCC/C	27.02	35.63	40.93	44.39	47.56	48.78	49.98	50.64	52.17	53.05	53.79	54.57	55.19	55.90	55.90
Investment grade	0.11	0.31	0.54	0.85	1.18	1.51	1.81	2.10	2.37	2.65	2.91	3.12	3.34	3.55	3.81
Speculative grade	4.65	9.22	13.28	16.59	19.18	21.33	23.11	24.55	25.86	26.99	28.01	28.86	29.69	30.38	31.04
All rated	1.61	3.21	4.66	5.90	6.92	7.80	8.52	9.14	9.70	10.22	10.69	11.08	11.47	11.83	12.20

Source: Diane Vazza, Devi Aurora and Ryan Schneck, Standard & Poor's Global Fixed Income Research and Standard & Poor's CreditPro® 7.02. "Annual 2005 Global Corporate Default Study and Ratings Transitions", January 2006. This chart is reproduced with the permission of Standard & Poor's Rating Services, a division of The McGraw-Hill Companies, Inc.

Standard & Poor's Long-Term Credit Ratings Definitions

AAA	An obligation rated 'AAA' has the highest rating we assign. The obligor's capacity to meet its financial commitment on the obligation is extremely strong.
AA	An obligation rated 'AA' differs from the highest-rated obligations only to a small degree. The obligor's capacity to meet its financial commitment on the obligation is very strong.
A	An obligation rated 'A' is somewhat more susceptible to the adverse effects of changes in circumstances and economic conditions than obligations in higher rated categories. However, the obligor's capacity to meet its financial commitment on the obligation is still strong.
BBB	An obligation rated 'BBB' exhibits adequate protection parameters. However, adverse economic conditions or changing circumstances are more likely to lead to a weakened capacity of the obligor to meet its financial commitment on the obligation.
BB	An obligation rated 'BB' is less vulnerable to nonpayment than other speculative issues. However, it faces major ongoing uncertainties or exposure to adverse business, financial, or economic conditions that could lead to the obligor's inadequate capacity to meet its financial commitment on the obligation.
B	An obligation rated 'B' is more vulnerable to nonpayment than obligations rated 'BB', but the obligor currently has the capacity to meet its financial commitment on the obligation. Adverse business, financial, or economic conditions likely will impair the obligor's capacity or willingness to meet its financial commitment on the obligation.
CCC	An obligation rated 'CCC' is vulnerable to nonpayment within one year, and depends on favorable business, financial, and economic conditions for the obligor to meet its financial commitment on the obligation. In the event of adverse business, financial, or economic conditions, the obligor is unlikely to have the capacity to meet its financial commitment on the obligation.
CC	An obligation rated 'CC' currently is highly vulnerable to nonpayment.
C	The 'C' rating is also used when a bankruptcy petition has been filed or similar action has been taken but payments on this obligation are being continued. 'C' is also used for a preferred stock that is in arrears (as well as for junior debt of issuers rated 'CCC-' and 'CC').
D	Default: 'SD': Selective default. The 'D' and 'SD' ratings, unlike other ratings, are not prospective; rather, they are used only when a default actually has occurred--not when default is only expected.

Note: Obligations rated 'BB', 'B', 'CCC', 'CC', and 'C' are regarded as having significant speculative characteristics. 'BB' indicates the least degree of speculation, and 'C' the highest. While such obligations likely will have some quality and protective characteristics, these may be outweighed by large uncertainties or major exposure to adverse conditions.

Source: Solomon B. Samson, Neri Bukspan and Emmanuel Dubois-Pelerin, Corporate Ratings Criteria 2008. "Long-Term Issue Credit Ratings Definitions", April 2008. This chart is reproduced with the permission of Standard & Poor's Rating Services, a division of The McGraw-Hill Companies, Inc.

that often choose to not be rated due to the associated expenses. That does not mean that the credit quality of the non-rated municipality is weak; it just means that without some research, you just don't know.

Figure 36   Moody's Weighted Average Cumulative Corporate Default Rates

Rating	Year 1	Year 5	Year 10
Aaa	0.0000	0.0995	0.5208
Aa	0.0078	0.1774	0.5225
A	0.0207	0.4720	1.2870
Baa	0.1815	1.9384	4.6366
Ba	1.2049	10.2153	19.1176
B	5.2361	26.7936	43.3426
Caa-C	19.4758	52.6218	69.1778

Notes: Moody's-rated only, 1970-2006 (%)

Source: Richard Cantor & Naomi Richmond, *Moody's Rating Methodology*, "The U.S. Municipal Bond Rating Scale: Mapping to the Global Rating Scale and Assigning Global Scale Ratings to Municipal Obligations", March 2007.

Moody's Long-Term Obligation Ratings

Aaa - Obligations rated Aaa are judged to be of the highest quality, with minimal credit risk.

Aa - Obligations rated Aa are judged to be of high quality and are subject to very low credit risk.

A - Obligations rated A are considered upper-medium grade and are subject to low credit risk.

Baa - Obligations rated Baa are subject to moderate credit risk. They are considered medium-grade and as such may possess certain speculative characteristics.

Ba - Obligations rated Ba are judged to have speculative elements and are subject to substantial credit risk.

B - Obligations rated B are considered speculative and are subject to high credit risk.

Caa - Obligations rated Caa are judged to be of poor standing and are subject to very high credit risk.

Ca - Obligations rated Ca are highly speculative and are likely in, or very near, default, with some prospect of recovery of principal and interest.

C - Obligations rated C are the lowest rated class of bonds and are typically in default, with little prospect for recovery of principal or interest.

Note: Moody's long-term obligation ratings are opinions of the relative credit risk of fixed-income obligations with an original maturity of one year or more. They address the possibility that a financial obligation will not be honored as promised. Such ratings reflect both the likelihood of default and any financial loss suffered in the event of default.

Source: Moody's Online Investor Services, www.moodys.com, July 2008.

In situations where ratings do not exist, investors should focus on factors such as the mix of industries in the municipality (essentially, look at the diversification of the tax base) and the source of the repayment of the bond. In the municipal bond universe, bonds usually rely on repayment either from the general ability of the municipality to levy and collect taxes, or the revenue generated from a specific project or entity. These bonds are typically called "general obligation bonds" and "revenue bonds," respectively. Figure 37 summarizes the key differences between these two types of bonds.

Figure 37   Basic Municipal Bond Types

Type	Repayment Source	Safety
General Obligation Bonds (G.O.)	• Municipalities taxing authority • Repaid from general tax receipts	• Usually fairly safe
Revenue Bonds	• Issued to fund a specific project. • Revenue for repayment comes from the specific project.	• Riskier as it is dependent on the success of the project.

Source: Author Analysis

CREDIT ENHANCEMENT

One way that issuers of either general obligation or revenue bonds improve the quality of their bonds is to buy insurance. Several companies offer insurance to municipalities that guarantee the return of principal to bond owners. The credit rating of the insurance company effectively becomes the rating on the bond that has this insurance. This insurance can provide the investor with an added level of protection and peace of mind while allowing the municipality to borrow money at lower rates.

The most common municipal bond insurers are Municipal Bond Insurance Association (MBIA) and Financial Guaranty Insurance Company (FGIC). These are for-profit companies, not affiliated with the government. It is important that investors realize that the insurance provided by these companies is not guaranteed by the government. The risk is that the insurers could experience problems themselves; they are not immune from potential downgrades. Even with credit enhancement, investors still need to look at the quality of the bond without the enhancement.

THE MATH

The best way to show how to evaluate tax-exempt bonds with taxable bonds is to show some hypothetical examples. Here we go:

Example A: An investor lives in Minnesota and has a federal tax rate of 35 percent and a state tax rate of 8 percent. This investor is faced with evaluating three investment options. All of them have the same maturity and all are rated "AAA":

1. A U.S. Treasury bond with a yield of 4.75 percent
2. A General Electric corporate bond with a yield of 5.30 percent
3. A Minnesota general obligation municipal bond with a yield of 3.75 percent

Which one is the best option? In order to answer this question, let's walk through the math on each of these alternatives and evaluate them all on the same basis—their fully taxable equivalent yield.

1. The U.S. Treasury bond has no state taxes, but will be subject to federal taxes. Take the interest rate of the bond, 4.75 percent, and divide by one minus the state tax rate. In this example, the math becomes 4.75 percent divided by .92, which equals 5.16 percent. This is the fully taxable equivalent yield of the bond.
2. The General Electric bond is a corporate bond and is subject to both state and federal taxes. As such, there is no calculation required; the 5.30 percent rate is the taxable equivalent yield.
3. Since the investor in this example is a Minnesota resident, the investor will not be subject to either state or federal taxes on the income from the Minnesota general obligation municipal bond. This is called a double tax-exempt situation. The calculation for this is a little more complicated because state income taxes reduce your taxable income at the federal level since they are an itemized deduction. In order to calculate the true value of the state tax exemption, you must first take the state tax rate and multiply by one minus the federal tax rate. In this example, that would reduce your state tax rate impact from 8 percent to 5.2 percent for purposes of calculating the taxable equivalent yield. The rest of the calculation looks like this:

$$\frac{3.75*}{1 - (\text{Fed tax rate} + \text{modified state tax rate})}$$

*The tax-exempt rate

The result of this calculation is a 6.27 percent taxable equivalent yield. So, for this investor, the Minnesota general obligation municipal bond generates the highest taxable equivalent yield and is therefore the best option for the investor based on yield.

Example B: An investor lives in Nevada and is in the 32 percent federal tax bracket. Nevada has no state income tax. The investor is faced with two different investment options with twelve-year maturities. The twist here is that the government agency bond is callable in five years.

1. California municipal bond paying 4.0 percent
2. Government agency bond paying 5.50 percent, but callable in five years; yield to the call date is 5.25 percent

First of all, let's explain a "call." A call means that the issuer of the bond can redeem the bond prior to maturity on a preset date and usually at a preset price. The investor then must look at the yield of the bond to the call date and the yield of the bond to the maturity date when evaluating the bond. Generally, the issuer will only call a bond when it is disadvantageous to the investor. What does that mean? If interest rates go down, the issuer may decide to redeem the bond and issue another bond at a lower interest rate, thereby saving some interest expense. The investor then must find another bond, probably at a lower interest rate, reducing his or her income in the process.

Why, then, would you ever consider a callable bond? There are many potential reasons. The issuer generally has to pay a higher level of interest in order to compensate the investor for the uncertainty of the length of time that he or she will receive the stated interest rate. Another reason could be that you believe it is unlikely the bond will be called based on the supply of other bonds outstanding from the issuer at even higher rates. Furthermore, you could think that interest rates will not fall, and you could handle the potential reduction in income if you turned out to be wrong.

As far as the evaluation of the two bonds in Example B goes, only one calculation needs to be done to compare the yield of the California bond to that of the agency bond. Simply take the 4 percent California bond yield and divide by one minus the Federal tax rate. This would result in a "taxable equivalent yield" of 5.88 percent for the California bond, which would be superior to the agency bond at final maturity.

HEIGHT AND WEIGHT TABLES, BENCHMARKS, AND TRACKING ERRORS

Some people are obsessed with tracking their weight on a daily basis. A wide variety of scales from the simple to the complex are available if we want to do that. In addition, tables that show us our ideal weight at various heights and ages are also available so we can compare ourselves to what is considered the standard at each time.

When investing, it is important to determine early on what the standard will be. While you shouldn't obsess about it on a daily basis, you do need some way to evaluate how your investments are doing. Investment advisors will often refer to these potential standards as "benchmarks."

The industry generally uses benchmarks that are, in many respects, irrelevant for private investors. It is common in the investment industry to use benchmarks of various stock market indices to measure your portfolio's success. Some of the more popular ones are the DJIA or the S&P 500. Why do you care that your portfolio is tracked against these benchmarks? Most investors have goals that are not closely aligned with these indices. For example, many investors have a goal to beat inflation by 2 or 3 percent on an annual basis.

Other investors have a goal to achieve a stated annual return, say 6 percent per year in their portfolios. These goals are usually rooted in some rationale. In the first example, perhaps it's a desire to keep their purchasing power intact and with a modest growth in purchasing power over time. In the second example, it may be that the investor can satisfy his or her goal of a 6 percent return per year from his or her portfolio. What does this have to do with the DJIA or the S&P 500? Nothing.

Even though you should not track your portfolio against market indices, it is often useful to track individual funds or managers within your portfolio against these indices. When using market indices to evaluate a specific fund or manager, be sure to use a long enough timeframe to give a true indication of manager performance rather than simple good or bad luck. I suggest a minimum of five years, but ten years would be even better.

A study by the research firm, Litman/Gregory Research, indicated that nearly every large company manager it tracked that had a ten-year record of outperformance over his or her benchmark went through a three-year period where he or she underperformed the benchmark by at least 2 percent points per year. Someone evaluating performance on a three-year timeframe is going to have trouble finding managers who outperform in the long run.

Another element of performance and comparisons to a benchmark is the issue of tracking error. It is important to understand how closely a given manager or fund can be expected to track a benchmark over shorter time periods. This variance from the benchmark is referred to as tracking error. (A more complete discussion of tracking error can be found in the Glossary section of this book.)

A manager with a high degree of tracking error allows you to potentially generate returns in excess of the benchmark over time. Yet, a manager with a high tracking error will undergo short-term time periods when, quite bluntly, he or she will look stupid. If you are concerned that you will not have the patience to stick with a manager with high tracking error over the long haul, you may be better off with a manager who hugs the index. This is contrary to what many advisors will tell you. They will say that hugging the index will give you returns very close to the benchmark over time. Okay, that may not be exciting, but it is better than the returns that investors experience on average (see Chapter 5).

Again, from a portfolio perspective, an investor should generally try to find a benchmark that measures how you are tracking toward your goals. If you or your advisor have established a goal, and then determined that you need to generate 6 percent annually to achieve your goal, then 6 percent becomes your benchmark. Potential portfolio benchmarks are illustrated in Figure 38.

In an investor survey completed in August 2010, the majority of investors said they preferred benchmarks that related to either absolute dollar returns or absolute percentage returns (see Figure 39). Fund managers and other investment professionals often get overly fixated on performance relative to some industry benchmark or peer group even though most individual investors are simply more concerned with the dollar value of their portfolio over time.

Figure 38   Portfolio Benchmarks

GOAL	BENCHMARK
Maintain purchasing power/Capital preservation	CPI* + 3%
Achieve investment plan goal	Absolute return target – example of 6%
Achieve investment plan goal	Absolute dollar growth of portfolio
Achieve income goal (possible spending goal)	Combined income and dividend target

* CPI is Consumer Price Index – a commonly used measure of inflation.

Source: Author Analysis

Figure 39   Investor Preferences for Performance Measurement

Absolute Dollar Value Change	50%
Return Above a Minimally Acceptable Level	24%
Return Relative to Industry Benchmark (i.e. S&P 500)	26%

Healthy Investment Tips

1. Schedule and plan a thorough portfolio review every year.
2. Do the math to determine if you are better off with taxable bonds or tax-exempt bonds.
3. Understand the credit quality and call features of your bonds.
4. High ratings from rating agencies are not an assurance that losses will not occur, especially during periods of severe market stress.
5. Utilize an appropriate performance benchmark that is helpful to you in measuring how you are doing relative to your investment goals.

14

The Importance of Strong Bones: Zigs and Zags

Bones: The calcified connective tissues that form the skeleton of the body

Most health care professionals I have talked to cite the importance of keeping your bones strong, especially as you age. There are numerous actions you can take to help yourself in this regard, including proper exercise and nutrition. Our bones are critical to our bodies because they are the support structures that hold everything together. Likewise, diversification is the support structure for an investment portfolio.

We have already touched on the importance of diversification and maintaining the proper balance in your portfolio. Now it is time to go a little deeper and explain how this works. Many investment professionals refer to this as ensuring that your investments have low correlation relative to each other. In simple terms, this means that you want to have assets in your portfolio that zig when others zag. I am not sure if "zig" means they go up and "zag" means they go down, but let's assume that for the moment.

An investor recently asked me why one would want to do that; he asked why one would not want all of his or her investments to zig, or go up, and that is a very good question. Here's the answer: If you knew with certainty that every investment in your portfolio would go up, then you would not need to worry about diversification. The problem is that no one knows, and if someone tells you he or she does, steer clear of that person! The key is to find investments that react differently to different stimuli in the economy and the world, and then mix them together to create a portfolio that will give you a high probability of meeting your objectives over time.

Examples of investments and how they may react to different stimuli are described in Figure 40.

You can see from this simple chart that you probably need some exposure to commodities and real estate in your portfolio to defend against inflation. You need international exposure to defend against—or take advantage of—a weak dollar. You need bonds to take advantage of slow growth and stocks to take advantage of fast growth. This is an overly simplistic view, and over various time periods, these relationships may not hold true. During periods of extreme market volatility, it is not unusual for different asset categories to exhibit high correlations with each other.

A common mistake made by U.S. investors is believing that diversification means owning thirty to forty good U.S. companies. Even if these companies are diversified across economic industry sectors, the table on zigs and zags reveals the problems with this approach. Certainly, the thirty- or forty-stock portfolio can help an investor mitigate the impact that a couple of bad stock picks could have, but not much else. When the stock market is under severe

Figure 40   Zigs and Zags

Investment Type	High Inflation	Slow Growth	Fast Growth	Weak Dollar
U.S. Bonds	ZAG	ZIG	ZAG	ZAG
Foreign Bonds	ZAG	ZIG	ZAG	ZIG
U.S. Stocks	ZAG	ZAG	ZIG	ZIG/ZAG
Foreign Stocks	ZAG	ZAG	ZIG	ZIG
Commodities	ZIG	ZAG	ZIG	ZIG
Real Estate	ZIG	ZIG/ZAG	ZIG/ZAG	ZIG/ZAG

Key: "Zig" – goes up; "Zag" – goes down

Source: Author Analysis

stress due to various reasons, most stocks go down. Having thirty or five hundred makes little difference in the resulting loss of principal. In times like those, investors see the value of having some bonds, some real estate, some commodities, and other investments not influenced to the same degree by the same factors that move stocks.

Again, human anatomy is an interesting guide with the body containing more than two hundred different bones—each bone fulfilling a purpose for the good of the whole body.

Investment professionals look at the degree to which different investments either zig or zag relative to each other. This is called "correlation." The correlation measure shows the degree to which one investment moves in tandem with another investment. Figure 41 shows correlation data for many different asset classes.

Generally speaking, the lower the correlation number, the less correlated an investment is to another investment. This is what you should consider when looking for good diversifiers in your portfolio. It is important to note that just because an investment has a low correlation to another investment, it does not mean that it has lower risk. On a standalone basis, it may be *very* risky, and

Figure 41   Correlation of Returns

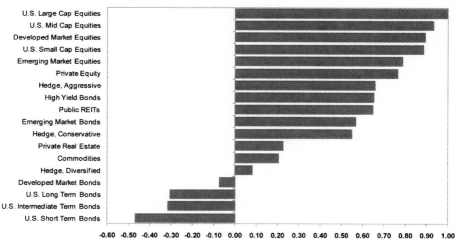

U.S. Large Cap Equities vs. Other Asset Classes

March 1990 to March 2011
Data Source: MorningStar EnCorr, June 2011
© 2011 Wells Fargo Bank, N.A. All rights reserved. Used with permission from Wells Fargo Bank, N. A.

unless you are a sophisticated investor, it may be difficult for you to find that right mix. An investment professional who utilizes an asset allocation discipline can help you find the right mix of investments for your situation.

The globalization of world economies and the increased access to different types of assets for investors has tended to bring correlations more closely together for certain asset types. In addition to the correlation data, it is important for investors to ask themselves, "Do I have investments in my portfolio that will react differently in different economic environments?" Additionally, investors need to consider how different country dynamics will impact those investments (e.g., government policies, taxation, currency trends, etc.).

Figure 41 illustrates that the closer the number is to zero, the less correlation. For example, developed market bonds have a negative number on this chart. This implies that they tend to move in the opposite direction of stocks. In other words, if stocks go down, developed market bonds typically go up. If you think about the earlier table with the economic forces, and how they impact different asset classes, it makes sense. It may be a slow global growth environment that is causing stocks to retreat, but developed market bonds tend to do well in that environment.

You can also see from this chart the value that bonds can provide—especially short maturity bonds—from a diversification standpoint. I often hear investors who are oriented toward growth ask, "Why do I need any bonds in my portfolio?" The low correlation of short-term bonds to stocks answers at least part of that question. They are simply great portfolio diversifiers (and they also provide a consistent stream of income to the investor).

Healthy Investment Tips

1. Maintain proper diversification and balance in your portfolio.
2. Include assets in your portfolio that zig when others zag.
3. Even growth-oriented investors may benefit from holding some short-maturity bonds in their portfolios for income and diversification reasons.

15

Choosing Your Doctor: Selecting the Right Investment Advisor

Selection: A process to determine and arrive at a choice

While I do not claim to be an expert on how people pick their doctors, my guess is that it is often done by chance. Most people want a primary doctor located close to where they live, so they check out a nearby clinic and inquire as to when they can get in to see someone. Often the first available appointment becomes a driving factor on the actual doctor selection.

Chances are pretty good that the doctor they get will be a general practitioner. In many respects, that doctor will be an entry point into the vast world of health care. From that point, the new patient may get referred to a specialist who can help deal with more specific health issues. The degree to which the specialist reports back, collaborates, and communicates with the primary doctor varies.

Some of the top clinics in the world now use a generalist doctor, who will then surround you with a team of specialists, should you need one. To some degree, the best clinical models are being replicated in the investment advisory business. A team of specialists is often available to a generalist advisor, depending on the needs and complexity of the investor. Much has already been written about how to choose an investment advisor. Because of this, I will take a different path and focus first on the question you must ask yourself: *What do I want my advisor to do?*

QUESTIONS TO ASK YOURSELF

Here are some potential questions to ask yourself before beginning a search for an investment advisor. These questions will help you focus your search for the right type of advisor for you:

1. Do I want someone to craft an overall investment plan for me?
2. In addition to crafting a plan, do I also want someone to execute that plan?
3. Do I want to execute the plan myself?
4. Do I simply want someone to bounce ideas off from time to time (i.e., a sounding board)?
5. Do I want to execute the plan myself, but need someone to provide me with a steady flow of ideas?
6. Do I want someone to help keep me disciplined to my overall investment plan?
7. Do I just want to turn over my investments to someone else and have that person do it all while just keeping me updated periodically on how my investment portfolio is tracking to my plan?
8. Am I the kind of person who will not be able to give up day-to-day control of my investment decisions?
9. Do I want to be educated on investments?
10. Am I disinterested in investments to the point where I don't really want to be bothered by any of this?
11. Am I interested in investments, but just don't have the time to do it myself?
12. How do I want to compensate my advisor? Commission on every idea? Fees on assets managed? Hourly advice charges?

Once you have asked these questions and understand what you want your advisor to do, then you can begin your search. The first step is to develop a list of potential advisors.

How the list of potential advisors is developed depends, to some extent, on how you answer the questions above. If, for example, you are looking for someone to create an investment plan for you, but you will be executing that plan on your own, a list of fee-only financial planners is what you need to create. If you are looking for someone to provide you with a steady stream of ideas, you may be looking for a full-service broker at a large brokerage firm or bank with access to a wide range of product ideas.

Figure 42 is a helpful guide to assembling the list of potential advisors. The next step in the process is to do due diligence on each advisor on your list. A good place to start is to examine the following three characteristics of each advisor: their credentials, training, and experience.

TYPES OF ADVISORS AND WHERE TO FIND THEM

An advisor's credentials and training will relate to the type of advisor he or she is. Many credentials are quite easy to obtain and have no prerequisite for any actual investment experience.

There is an entire industry that has developed around the creation of credentials, and you need to understand how, if at all, the credentials benefit you. Ask your potential advisor what his or her credentials actually mean, what the prerequisites are for obtaining them, and how he or she went about obtaining them. You should also ask the advisor to provide you with a website that can give you more information on those credentials.

Figure 42 Finding an Advisor

What Will the Advisor Do?	Best Advisor Type?	Where to Find?
Create a Plan	Fee-only financial planner	College of Financial Planning
Execute a Plan	Money Manager/Broker	Referrals, Bank, Brokerage Firm
Generate Ideas	Full-service broker	Bank or large Brokerage Firm
Handle Everything	Money Manager/Broker	Bank or large Brokerage Firm

Source: Author Analysis

If you decide to use a financial planner, the preferred credential is often the certified financial planner (CFP) designation. This designation is earned after the successful completion of financial planning coursework that often takes two to three years to complete. In addition to the coursework, advisors must also successfully complete a ten-hour exam before they can use the credential.

An advisor with the CFP designation should be able to help you craft an overall financial and investment plan, but may or may not be someone you would use to manage your money, depending on his or her other experience and expertise. I also caution you to be aware of investment product salespeople cloaked in the title of financial planner. Some planners accept commissions, loads, and other fees from investment products that they recommend to you. Make sure you understand what conflicts they may have, and be sure that they are being objective in recommending investments for your portfolio.

If you decide to use a broker, he or she must be securities-licensed, having what is typically referred to as a Series 7 license. This can be achieved through coursework covering a variety of investment topics and regulations, culminating in the successful completion of a six-hour exam. Many brokers earn additional licenses that provide them with a base of knowledge in areas such as supervision of other brokers, the use of options and futures contracts, research report writing, and insurance.

Brokers interested in managing money for investors in a fee-base environment rather than a transaction structure will often earn a credential such as the certified investment management analyst (CIMA) designation. This designation is earned after the successful completion of coursework and an exam covering areas such as asset allocation, research analysis, and performance measurement. In addition, many brokers are becoming more active in a planning role and are earning the CFP designation to help them with their knowledgebase in that area.

A professional money manager (typically called a "portfolio manager" or "investment manager"), will often hold a chartered financial analyst (CFA) charter. This is earned after the successful completion of a three-year program that requires you to study for and pass three levels of exams. In order to hold a CFA designation, the individual must have at least three years of investment management or investment analysis experience.

Once you have developed a list of five or six potential advisors located in your city (if a local presence is important to you), and who appear to have the credentials, training, and experience you prefer, then you can continue your due diligence. This simply means doing some background research on the potential advisors to be sure they all have the experience, training, reputation, trustworthiness, and squeaky-clean records you are looking for.

Make sure you check to see that the advisors have the credentials and licenses that they claim to have, and that their credentials or licenses are not under any review or suspension due to potentially improper conduct. You can check with the appropriate sponsoring organization (National Association of Securities Dealers for brokers, CFA Institute for CFAs, Investment Management Consultants Association for CIMAs, and Certified Financial Planner Board of Standards for CFPs) to inquire on those issues.

If the advisor works for a firm that is a registered investment advisor company (i.e., firms generally managing more than $25 million in assets), you should ask for a copy of Form ADV. This form lists important information about the advisor, his or her education, and employment history, as well as the services offered and fees charged. Bank trust departments can provide you with bios and fee schedules; they are not required to register as investment advisors because they are regulated by the Office of the Comptroller of the Currency (OCC) and held to fiduciary investment standards.

THE "LOOK ELSEWHERE" FACTORS

There are some issues that may surface while you're busy researching information about your potential advisor. I call these issues the "look elsewhere" factors. If you run into any of these red flags, cross off that potential advisor from your list and look elsewhere.

Chemistry and honesty are two key look elsewhere factors to consider. If the advisor you interview starts telling you what you should do before getting to know you and your situation, look elsewhere. If an advisor tells you how he or she has a foolproof process or system to beat the market or generate above-market returns, look elsewhere. If he or she "guarantees" anything, look elsewhere.

I have been involved in several requests for proposals (RFPs), a competitive process where an investor gathers information on several different advisors or firms to potentially hire as his or her investment advisor. In one of the RFPs, the question was asked of potential advisors, "What type of market environment would you expect to outperform, and under what conditions would you expect to underperform the U.S. equity market?" I came back with the answer that we would expect to underperform when the equity market in the U.S. was going straight up, and we would expect to outperform when the market was very volatile and/or going down. Later, the consultant told me that out of several advisors/firms that answered this question, I was the only one who did not say that we would outperform in any environment. I believe this was important in winning the business. Honesty really does matter.

Another factor you should explore is the number of clients an advisor serves and the type of service you can expect from him or her. Ask for some references from his or her existing clients. Then call those clients and find out what kind of service, contact, and advice they receive. Make sure that it is consistent with what you would expect of an advisor. An advisor who is able and willing to communicate with you, the investor, in a way you prefer with the frequency you need is a critical element in the success of your working relationship. If not, look elsewhere.

Furthermore, ask for an evaluation of how the advisor gets paid. Ask what his or her annual fees are. Or, if he or she is paid on each transaction, what is the per-transaction fee? You may want to double-check this information with a credible source; oftentimes, advisors receive fees or commissions that come out of the return of the investment, but are not explicitly paid by the investor. In many cases, advisors present this as no charge to you. I do not know any advisors who work for free, so if they imply that there is no charge for their services, look elsewhere.

An important, but often overlooked issue with picking an advisor is the care in which he or she transitions your existing portfolio to a recommended portfolio. Many advisors want to blow out your existing portfolio right away and move into the portfolio they recommend. It is not likely that every investment you purchased was a dumb idea and not at all appropriate to your goals.

Generally, liquidating at least a portion of your portfolio makes sense. However, when an advisor wants to sell your entire portfolio, it is to make it easy on himself or herself or because he or she does not have the resources or expertise to follow any of your existing investments. Even if a transition plan ends up recommending a substantial restructuring of your portfolio, there needs to be consideration given to taxes, transaction costs, and fees to exit certain investments that could extend the transition over multiple years. If you are getting pushed really hard to sell your entire portfolio immediately, and with no consideration to these factors, look elsewhere.

An important area to explore with any potential investment advisor relates to his or her investment philosophy and process. What is the advisor's investment philosophy? Does it match your own? Does it resonate with you? Does it make sense? Also, ask about the investment process. What is the advisor's process? If a potential advisor cannot clearly articulate philosophy and process, it is likely he or she does not have one. Guess what? You should look elsewhere.

Firm size and type can be an important factor when choosing an advisor. An advisor associated with a small firm may not have the breadth of investment products and services that you need or desire. He or she may also not have access to a wide range of idea flow that larger firms may be able to provide. Ask to see a list of investment options that will be available to you should you become a client. Also, check the degree to which the advisor offers significant choices between proprietary products and non-proprietary products. Proprietary products are generally manufactured and managed by the firm, and non-proprietary products are manufactured and managed by an external firm. It is usually good to have a blend of both available.

Firm type comes into play when dealing with firms that have natural biases. For example, advisors working at insurance companies often find only insurance solutions to be the best fit for their clients. Advisors of mutual fund companies often find proprietary mutual funds to be the right solution. In either case, these may be very good options; just make sure you understand *why* they are being recommended to you.

Small or boutique-style investment firms are often well-known for great customer service, but may have a limited menu of investment offerings. This limited menu of investment offerings can sometimes result in a limited asset allocation and portfolio construction framework for the investor. If you work with a small firm like this, one of the first questions you should ask your advisor is to see the range of investment options and the range of asset classes and sub-asset classes that he or she can utilize in the construction of your portfolio. If the firm has partnered with another company to get access to a broader set of solutions, this concern could be mitigated.

Another firm or advisor consideration is how much experience the firm or advisor has in dealing with individual investors. Many firms, and some advisors, focus their practice on institutional clients. If they do, it is possible that they will not fully understand or appreciate the nuances of individual investors. An example of this may be their unwillingness to customize portfolios to each investor's unique needs. Another example may be the lack of consideration to the importance of taxes to the individual investor and the need to structure portfolios with tax efficiency in mind. It is also possible that institutional firms/advisors will not get that individual investors are often more focused on downside risk protection than institutional investors. If any of this seems to describe an advisor or a firm you are considering, look elsewhere.

Over time, I have seen investors place a high degree of importance on picking advisors based on the following three key factors:

1. A referral from a trusted source
2. The breadth of products and services offered
3. The firm's reputation

Getting a referral from someone you trust or from someone you know at a firm that focuses on individual investors can be a great place to start your search for an advisor.

Healthy Investment Tips

1. Before starting down the path of finding an advisor, figure out what you want the advisor to do for you. Take the time to conduct a self-assessment of the role you want an advisor to play. Use the list of questions outlined in this chapter.
2. Once you have figured out what you want your advisor to do, start putting together a list of potential advisors who fit your needs.
3. Thoroughly research the background of the advisors you are interviewing. Check regulatory records, credentials, experience, and references.
4. If you can get a referral from a trusted source, this can be an added benefit in your search for an advisor.
5. Understand the advisor's investment philosophy and process, and make sure it is a good match with your own beliefs.
6. Make sure there is chemistry between you and your advisor. You want an advisor you can get along with, but you also want one who will challenge you and not just agree with everything you say.

16

Discipline: Good for the Body, Good for the Portfolio

Discipline: The ability to conduct self-control

Too many investors suffer from "short-termitis." They lack either the patience or the discipline to stick with investments in which they originally believed. This is true regardless of the type of investment vehicles owned by an investor. Holders of individual stocks, mutual funds, and separate account managers can all have the potential to suffer from their own short-term focus.

Most investment experts would agree that you should probably not invest in stocks unless you have at least a five-year time horizon. I believe you need at least a ten-year time horizon to allow recovery time from a potential bear market on the front-end of this timeframe. I referenced this minimum ten-year time horizon in the original version of my book before the bear market of 2008 to 2009. This bear market, combined with the 2000 to 2002 bear market, contributed to what was often referred to as "The Lost Decade" for stocks from 2000 through 2009. Prior to that, the last time an entire decade produced negative returns for U.S. stocks was in the 1930s. The total return was -0.5 percent for that decade.

An investor who was diversified across global stocks, bonds, real estate, and commodities enjoyed a positive return in both of these decades of negative U.S. stock returns. Once again, this once illustrates the importance of diversification across more than just one asset class. In spite of this, the following chart, Figure 43, from the NYSE, suggests that investors continue to be impatient.

The average stock was held for five years in 1973 and for three years in 1981. By 2008, however, the average stock was held for less than ten months! Individual investors should not take the full blame for this; hedge fund managers, program traders, and even mutual fund managers contribute to this data. This short investment-holding period makes it difficult for investors to realize the benefit that comes from holding stocks over the long run.

Since 2008, turnover of stocks has actually declined for the first time in almost twenty-five years. My hypothesis is that this improvement is due to many of the "most impatient" investors moving out of equities after the second bear market of the decade, leaving a higher proportion of patient long-term investors.

Figure 43   Turnover Rate for Listed Equities

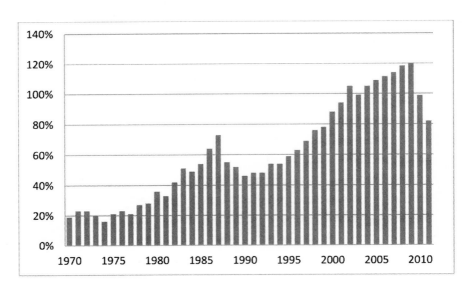

1970 through June of 2011, Data Source: NYSE, 2007

LIFE EXPECTANCY AND HOW THIS IMPACTS YOUR ASSET ALLOCATION

According to the U.S. Center for Health Statistics, a female can be expected to live to the age of eighty-and-a-half, and a male can be expected to live approximately seventy-five years. Life expectancy in the U.S. continues to increase as health care improves. So, why is this important? Simply put, the issue of life expectancy has a bearing on your investment time horizon. The investment time horizon, in turn, has a bearing on your asset allocation.

Not too many years ago, it was common for a male to retire from the workforce at sixty-five years of age and die at sixty-eight or sixty-nine. Women generally lived a few years longer. What this means is that the years in retirement were probably in the five- to seven-year range, and people only needed enough money to cover themselves for that length of time. They were also eligible to draw Social Security right away, and more than likely had a reasonably generous pension from their last employers. All of this has changed.

Now, it is not uncommon for workers to retire at sixty and live another twenty years or more—and often living that twenty-plus years without a defined benefit pension from an employer. From the life expectancy actuarial tables, we also learn that as we get older, our life expectancy extends even further. Essentially, if you beat the odds of death by accident or disease, your probability of living longer increases. So, for example, a sixty-year-old male has a life expectancy of approximately twenty more years, or just over five years more than his life expectancy at birth. Figure 44 gives some other data on this phenomenon.

The implications of this life expectancy data on your asset allocation are important. The old rules of thumb need to be reevaluated. First, the general idea that when you retire, you should shift most of your assets to bonds may not make sense in a world of longer life expectancies where inflation can gradually eat away at your purchasing power. The rule of thumb that says you should subtract your age from one hundred and use that number as the percentage of your portfolio to be invested in stocks also needs revisiting.

Figure 44   U.S. Life Expectancy

Current Age	Male (Caucasian)	Female (Caucasian)	Male (African-American)	Female (African-American)
At birth	75.7	80.6	69.7	76.5
30	47.3	51.5	42.4	48.2
40	37.9	41.9	33.5	38.9
50	29.0	32.6	25.2	30.2
60	20.9	23.8	18.2	22.2
70	13.6	15.9	12.3	15.1
75	10.5	12.3	9.8	12.0

Data Source: U.S. National Center for Health Statistics, Vital Statistics of the United States, annual; and National Vital Statistics Report (NVSR), Vol. 58, No. 21.

THE IMPACT OF INFLATION ON YOUR PORTFOLIO

Let's explore this rule of thumb using a sixty-year-old investor as an example. If you do the simple math and subtract sixty from one hundred, you get forty. That would mean the investor's portfolio would have 40 percent in stocks and presumably the other 60 percent in bonds.

Let's assume this sixty-year-old has a $1 million portfolio, and that the bonds in the portfolio generate a 5 percent level of income while the stocks generate dividends of 2 percent. This portfolio would produce approximately $38,000 of income on an annual basis using the 40 percent stock and 60 percent bond allocation. Hopefully, the stocks will generate some appreciation so that the portfolio will have some gains over and above the income. But for now, let's just stick with the income element of the portfolio.

After ten years, assuming 3.5 percent annual inflation, the $38,000 annual income really only has $26,950 purchasing power. This is an erosion of 41 percent in just ten years.

More than likely, however, it will not be that bad because the stocks will probably increase their dividends over time; let's assume it will lead to an 8 percent increase in dividends annually. Over the ten years, this would mean an increase of $9,271, offsetting a big portion of the $11,050 reduction in purchasing power that the portfolio lost to inflation.

Still, this investor loses purchasing power. If the inflation rate averaged 5 percent over the ten years instead of the 3.5 percent, the loss of purchasing power would be 63 percent for an additional $3,500 reduction in buying power income.

If we were to update this old rule of thumb and used 110 minus the age, we would have a stock allocation of 50 percent. This actually drops the initial level of income from $38,000 to $35,000, but protects that income better from inflation. The purchasing power of the $35,000 drops by $10,178, using the same assumptions we did in the first example. But, after adding back the growth in dividend flows from the stocks, we can add back $11,589 of income flow, more than offsetting the impact of general inflation.

My conclusion here is that if you are going to use old rules of thumb, make sure you do the math and factor in the purchasing power erosion effect of

Figure 45   Impact of Inflation and Asset Allocation on Portfolio Income

Inflation Rate	Asset Allocation Stocks/ Bonds	Annual Portfolio Income (Starting)	After 10 Years – Annual Portfolio Income (Adjusted for Purchasing Power Loss/Gain)	After 20 Years – Annual Portfolio Income (Adjusted for Purchasing Power Loss/Gain)
2.0%	40/60%	$38,000	$40,444	$54,861
2.0%	50/50%	$35,000	$40,301	$60,164
2.0%	60/40%	$32,000	$40,158	$65,466
3.5%	40/60%	$38,000	$36,221	$48,386
3.5%	50/50%	$35,000	$36,411	$54,200
3.5%	60/40%	$32,000	$36,592	$60,013
5.0%	40/60%	$38,000	$32,600	$43,610
5.0%	50/50%	$35,000	$33,076	$49,801
5.0%	60/40%	$32,000	$33,371	$55,992

Assuming: $1 million portfolio, 5% bond coupon, 8% annual stock dividend growth rate
Source: Author Analysis

inflation over time. Based on my analysis, increased life expectancy has updated the old rule of thumb to the new rule of 110. Additionally, a bond-only portfolio is not as conservative an option as many investors think because it does not protect the investor from inflation or interest rate risk. These are two risks, often ignored by investors, that can impact whether you will be eating ramen noodles at home with the heat set at 58 degrees or eating out at your favorite restaurant.

Healthy Investment Tips

1. Have at least a five-year time horizon, and preferably ten years, when investing in stocks.
2. Inflation is a critical factor that investors must consider when planning for their long-term income needs and the proper construction of their portfolios.
3. Increased life expectancy and the length of retirement is cause for reevaluating retirement asset allocations and old "rules of thumb."

17

Are You Only Eating American Food? The Case for International Investing

International: The involvement of more than one country

Many investors have been slow to embrace the reality that we live in a global economy. Even the companies that make up the S&P 500, which includes only U.S.-based companies, now derive a significant percent of their pre-tax operating income (and an even more meaningful percent of their revenue growth) from international operations. As a result of this transformation to a global economy, it makes sense to dedicate a section of this book to international and emerging markets investing.

WHY WORRY ABOUT INVESTING INTERNATIONALLY?

Probably the best reason I can provide for investing internationally is captured in Figure 46. The story is simply that emerging markets have emerged! Aggregate emerging market economies represent about one-half of the world's economic output. Growth rates in many of the emerging economies continue to be much higher than the developed world, providing the potential for future opportunities.

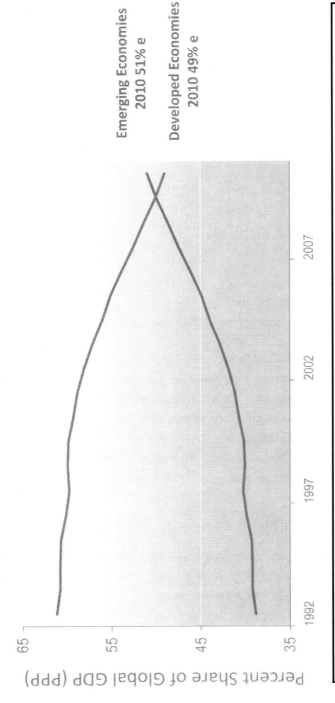

Figure 46   Emerging and Developed Economies Economic Output

Emerging Economies
2010 51% e

Developed Economies
2010 49% e

The Purchasing Power Parity (PPP) exchange rate is defined as the amount of currency that would be needed to purchase the same basket of goods and services as one unit of the reference currency, usually the US dollar.

In spite of the absolute level of economic activity that is now represented in emerging economies, many countries still have relatively low per capita gross domestic product (GDP). Figure 47 compares the per capita GDP of developed economies like the U.S. and Japan to emerging economies like China and India. You can easily see from this data that there is still potential for growth. South Korea is a good case study. Only thirty years ago, South Korea had similar per capita GDP as China does now; however, continued economic development and growth has propelled it much higher.

Growth opportunities in international and emerging market companies may significantly exceed those available in the U.S. at any given point in time. It makes little sense for individual investors in the U.S. to ignore this important growth element of the market. Companies based in the U.S. have seen this opportunity developing for years and have worked hard to take advantage of it. This is why nearly half the revenue of the companies that make up the S&P 500 comes from outside the U.S.—a number that will likely continue to grow over time. Many of these companies have, in effect, become global companies that happen to be headquartered in the U.S.

Figure 47   Selected Per Capita GDP by Country

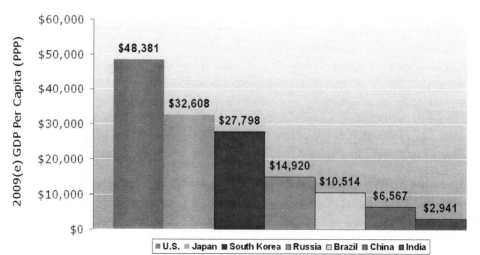

[1] *Gross domestic product based on purchasing-power-parity (PPP) per capita GDP, 2009 IMF estimates*

Data Source: IMF, World Economic Outlook, 4/10.

In Figure 48, you can see another reason for investing in international stocks—to position yourself for the shift that is taking place in economic production. In 1999, the U.S. produced approximately 24 percent of the entire world economic production, as measured by the GPD. By the end of 2007, this had dropped to approximately 21 percent. This is further evidence of the speed at which the economy is truly becoming global, an opportunity that will be at least partially missed by investors who focus only on their home country.

International investing does carry some unique risks. I believe that these risks primarily fall under one of two categories: currency or sovereign risk. Currency risk is the risk that the international country you are investing in may experience a depreciation of its currency relative to the U.S. dollar. This means that when you translate the investment back into U.S. dollars, you will likely lose money on that translation unless the value of the company went up more than the depreciation of the currency. This currency depreciation potential could be caused by many factors, including high rates of inflation, interest rate differentials between countries, government deficits, and other country-specific problems.

Sovereign risk is the risk of instability or, in rare cases, a default in the country in which you are investing. This could play out in the form of a coup where government control changes hands, causing uncertainty regarding the ownership of assets and companies. It could also be a country that just runs into some financial problems and cannot pay its debts. In either case, sovereign risk is a reason why you clearly want to be very diversified by country when you invest in emerging market economies.

THE DIFFERENCE BETWEEN DEVELOPED MARKETS AND EMERGING MARKETS

There are different technical definitions of developed markets and emerging markets. These countries have been identified generally based on their size, diversity of the economic base, political stability, and the sophistication and development of the country's infrastructure.

If you don't want to try to figure out the differences between developed and emerging countries yourself, you can rely on some commonly used indices. For example, Morgan Stanley has developed the MSCI EAFE Index, which is

Figure 48 The U.S. Share of Global GDP

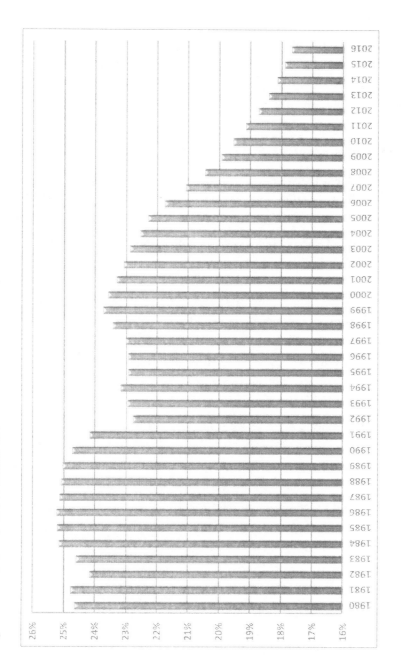

Data Source: International Monetary Fund
© 2011 Wells Fargo Bank, N.A. All rights reserved. Used with permission from Wells Fargo Bank, N. A.

an acronym for Morgan Stanley Capital International Europe, Australasia, and Far East. As its full name suggests, the MSCI EAFE Index represents Europe, Australasia, and the Far East. This index is generally thought of as representative of the developed international markets. Morgan Stanley also has an index for emerging markets called the MSCI Emerging Markets Index. The list of the countries making up these indices is included in Appendix IX.

FRONTIER MARKETS

Frontier markets are, in many ways, considered to be the "new emerging markets." By definition, frontier markets may not have robust or well-developed capital markets. Access to information on these markets may be limited. Investable opportunities and/or liquidity in investable opportunities may be limited in frontier markets.

Most investors should only consider accessing frontier markets through diversified funds with management and analysts who really understand these markets. Frontier markets represent a very high level of risk, but could present investors with a return that is above average and diversification benefits to other equity investments. As a result, this area may not be appropriate for many investors. At most, it should represent only a very small percentage of an investor's equity asset allocation.

Investors who want to have exposure to international stocks, bonds, or real estate must carefully consider their weightings if they use global funds. The word, "global," means "anywhere on the globe," including the U.S. In fact, I have seen global funds that have more than 50 percent of their exposure in the U.S. You will need to take that into consideration as you calculate your exposure to international markets. Global funds can be useful in a portfolio, but you will likely not get pure international exposure.

Investing in international bonds should generally only be attempted through diversified OEFs, CEFs, ETFs, or separately managed accounts. I highly recommend that investors not attempt to cherry pick a couple of international bonds to include in their bond portfolios. A couple of names will not provide you with sufficient diversification; it will only serve to increase risk in your portfolio.

Investors now have easier access to investments in emerging market fixed income funds. Emerging market fixed income funds can be accessed through ETFs, OEFs, CEFs, and separately managed accounts.

Benefits to investors in emerging market fixed income funds include further diversification of the income portion of their portfolios as well as potential currency diversification. Several options now exist for investors to invest in local currency emerging market fixed income funds, which is where the currency diversification element comes into play.

Some key considerations when investing in international bond funds include the following:

1. **The degree to which the manager hedges currency exposure.** Several funds in this space have hedged and unhedged versions available. Personally, I believe that a side benefit of owning international bond funds is getting exposure to investments that are denominated in currencies other than the U.S. dollar. If that is your view, you may want to consider unhedged options.

2. **Country exposure.** I would make sure you check to see how much exposure you have to bonds in an individual country. Some fund managers may stretch too much for yield and give you a high exposure to a country paying high rates, but take more risk in the process.

International real estate investing is another way to diversify your portfolio. This means investing in real estate outside of the U.S. As of the date of this writing, most U.S. investors who own real estate own *just* U.S. real estate. In the past, this made a lot of sense for investors; the U.S. real estate market is well-developed and has provided some excellent returns over the years. Even after the recent pullback, the returns have been stellar.

The means to effectively purchase international real estate has not been widespread until the last few years. Now, individual investors have the ability to purchase international real estate through mutual funds, ETFs, and private placement investments. I believe that investors will benefit from diversifying their real estate holdings globally, especially during periods of time when U.S. real estate is richly valued.

Healthy Investment Tips

1. If you are a U.S. investor, make sure to allocate and diversify a meaningful percent of your portfolio into international investments.
2. Understand the difference between developed markets and emerging markets. The growth possibilities, returns, and risks can be very different between these markets.
3. U.S. investors who fail to diversify their assets globally may miss out on better opportunities in the future.
4. Frontier markets are the "new" emerging markets and are likely to become more important in the future as a global stock market diversifier.

18

Staying Out of Trouble: Risk Control Strategies for the Individual Investor

Risk: The potential or likelihood of loss

One of the most important things an investor can do to meet his or her investment goals is to pay attention to risk. Investors have often exhibited a tendency to put more emphasis on returns than risk, yet the reverse is preferable. The reason is simple: A large negative drawdown on the portfolio caused by not understanding or paying attention to risk can take years from which to recover.

The two negative 50 percent bear markets in 2000 to 2009 swung the pendulum so that risk is now front and center of investors' minds—in some cases to the exclusion of earning a return sufficient to meet their goals. Regardless of the position of the risk pendulum at any given point in time, it is without doubt one of the most important issues that investors need to address.

ADDRESSING CONCENTRATION RISK

The first risk-control strategy I want to discuss revolves around addressing your concentrations. It has been said that concentrations are a great way to create wealth, but not to keep it. So what is a concentration? I typically define it as anything that represents more than 10 percent of your portfolio.

Many investors who work for a publicly traded company end up with a concentration of the stock in that company. It can be difficult, both practically and emotionally, to reduce such a holding to less than a 10 percent level, but an over-concentration does create a potential problem in that your paycheck and your wealth are significantly impacted by the same company. This can be good news—think of early investors in Microsoft or Apple—but it can also have a serious downside. Remember what happened with Enron or WorldCom?

If at all possible, try to limit your exposure to any one company to less than 10 percent of your portfolio. This should also be true for bonds, with the exception of U.S. Treasuries (although understanding country or sovereign risk is important as various countries struggle with issues like inflation, recessions, or budget challenges). You want to limit your exposure to any one corporate bond or any one municipality to less than 10 percent of your portfolio. This also applies to other asset classes such as real estate or specific commodities.

Another potential concentration risk can be economic sectors. Certainly the 10 percent limit can be exceeded from an overall industry perspective, as long as you are diversified within the industry. However, many investors think they are protected when they own several utility stocks instead of just one, or several bank stocks instead of just one. Yet, the same economic forces impact all companies in an industry. Too much exposure to one industry, and then encountering an industry-wide problem, could set you up for a large negative impact on your portfolio. Other types of concentration risks include geographic, currency, property, single manager, company size, style of manager, etc.

The following list can act as a guide to make sure you are at least evaluating potential concentrations in your portfolio.

Types Of Concentration Risk

- Individual stock
- Individual bond issuer
- Individual counterparty (guarantor of principal repayment, insurance, etc.)
- Economic industry

- Geographic (both within the country and globally)
- Currency in which investments are denominated
- Property type (e.g., in REITs, having all your exposure in apartments)
- Company size (large, medium, small, micro-cap)
- Investment style (growth and value)
- Credit risk (high-yield bond exposure)

MARKET RISK AND COMPANY RISK

Concentration risk at the company level is essentially the risk that a company-specific problem will cause the stock to drop. This risk is referred to as "company risk," or "company-specific risk." This risk is the whole reason why limiting your exposure to any one company is so important. Company-specific risk can be mitigated quite effectively by being diversified across a wide range of companies in different industries. Furthermore, company risk is significantly reduced once you have at least thirty names (across a broad range of industries) in a portfolio.

Figure 49   Market Risk Versus Company-Specific Risk

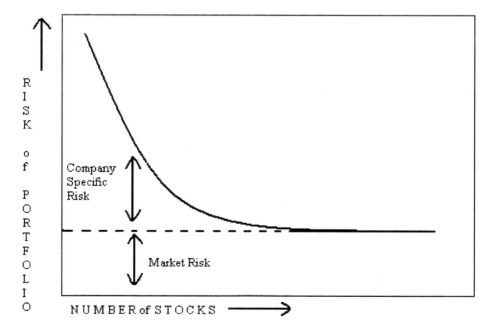

One problem that some investors face when dealing with company-specific risk is that they do not really know how much of any individual stock they truly own. If, for example, you own ten different mutual funds, it is difficult to keep track of similar names held across your funds. You may find out that six of these funds own General Electric stock. More than likely, you did not intend to own that much GE stock when you purchased the ten different mutual funds.

Fortunately, there is readily available software that has been designed to at least track the problem of single-stock redundancy in your fund holdings. Morningstar has a product that will give you a portfolio-level view of any stock you own in aggregate across your funds or money managers. This allows you to see what degree of company-specific risk you have taken on without even knowing it.

The chart that I just referenced also shows company risk in comparison to market risk. Market risk is the risk that the overall market could decline. Holding more names of individual stocks does not reduce this risk. It is also not mitigated by holding a large number of stock mutual funds. When the market experiences big downturns, most stocks go down; therefore, holding more names does not help that much. Market risk needs to be addressed in a different way.

There are several ways to protect against market risk: diversification of the portfolio into low or non-correlated asset classes relative to the stock market; structure your assets so your principal is protected; or employ hedging strategies. We have already discussed diversification. Bonds, real estate, and commodities are all asset classes that have relatively low correlation to stocks and can be used to mitigate the risk of a stock market pullback. Often investors make the mistake of thinking that by adding these asset classes they will somehow improve their overall short-run portfolio returns.

UNDERSTAND RISKS BEYOND VOLATILITY

Frequently, investments have risks well beyond the traditional risk of volatility. Some of these additional risks may include items such as:

- Liquidity risk
- Leverage risk

- Event risk

- Operational risk

Investors should seek to understand all the risks that could impact their investments before constructing their portfolios or deciding to add a new investment to their portfolios.

Diversification is all about reducing risk, which, over the long run, may enhance overall portfolio return experience. But one should not give up on diversification just because the additional asset classes are not adding immediately to the performance of the overall portfolio; that would be missing the point.

We recently re-examined data on how long you need to hold stocks to have a positive return. Using data from 1926 through 2008, the answer is sixteen years for an all-equity portfolio. Yet, for a 50/50 balanced stock/bond portfolio, the timeframe drops to approximately seven years. Interestingly enough, you need a nine-year period to not have a negative return for an all-bond portfolio over that eighty-three-year timeframe. The chart below illustrates the importance of simple asset allocation over time.

Figure 50   Portfolios That Never Lost Money: 1926 to 2008

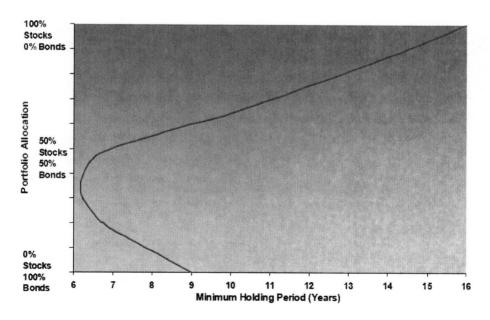

Data Source: Bloomberg Finance LLP, Factset, Wells Fargo Wealth Management, 02/09

I have found that it is quite common that the more volatile the performance of an investment portfolio, the greater the likelihood of an investor abandoning his or her long-term financial plan. In my view, utilizing broad asset class diversification that includes an appropriate exposure to stocks, bond, real assets, and complementary assets for your specific circumstances can potentially help smooth out bumps along the way. It can also help you stay on course. In addition, certain investment strategies and vehicles such as complementary strategies, risk-adjusted strategies, and principal-protected structures (where appropriate) can potentially help investors reduce their exposure to market risk.

Stop for a moment and note that in both cases mentioned above, I did not say "eliminate" the bumps or risk. Just as it is uncommon to be on an airplane and experience no turbulence throughout the flight, one should not expect to have a turbulence-free investment journey. I have never seen someone parachute out of an airplane at the first sign of turbulence.

It is important to understand where we are at in the cyclical process. Simply put, it is just that—a cycle. Below is a chart that is a good depiction of investors' emotions as the market goes through its cycle. As the market bottoms, capitulation turned to despondency. While it's important to recognize the fear that some investors may be experiencing at a point in time, it's even more important to realize where that point is in the context of the investor emotions cycle (see Figure 51).

Principal-protected structures are investments usually sold with a wrapper of a note or a certificate of deposit (CD) that allow an investor to have exposure to an asset class (usually via an index) over a set period of time. Typically, these investments have some level of principal protection. Principal protection of no more than 15 percent on notes with maturities longer than three years has a significant advantage for taxable investors because it allows them to use capital gains tax treatment on the returns and gain on the note. (Check with a tax advisor to make sure this rule has not changed). If investors buy these investments in a tax-qualified account, or are in a very low tax bracket, they may want to consider 100 percent principal protection, which is taxed at the ordinary tax rate of the investor.

Figure 51 Cycle of Investor Emotions

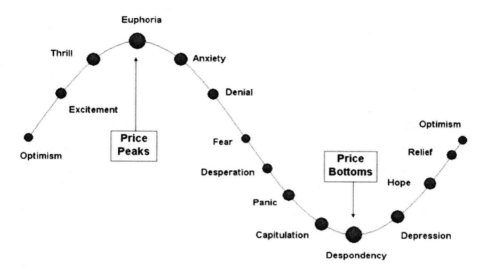

Hedging strategies can include a wide variety of instruments and approaches, including:

- **The use of put options.** Put options allow an investor to sell a security or basket of securities at a predetermined price within a preset time-frame regardless of market movements.

- **The use of a collar.** A collar allows an investor to essentially bracket the price around the current price. For example, if the price of a stock is $30, a collar may allow you to protect your downside risk in that stock if it fell below $25.50. In other words, $25.50 would be the worst you could do. In order to pay for that downside protection, a call is sold that essentially limits your upside potential profit in the stock. In this hypothetical example, that may be at a price of $33. So if the stock appreciated another 10 percent beyond its current level, you would still capture that return, but any appreciation above the 10 percent level would not be realized.

- **Sale of a covered call.** This strategy simply involves selling a call (an option to buy) on a stock that you already own at a predetermined price within a certain period of time. There are two basic types of call options:

    a. American; these may be exercised at any time prior to expiration; and

    b. European; these are exercisable only at expiration.

- **Fat-Tail Risk Hedging.** This is a relatively new concept where investors seek to establish a maximum drawdown target and then hedge against the target. For example, an investor might determine that the maximum downside exposure he or she can tolerate is 25 percent. The objective, then, is to cut off that potential tail by buying a protective put to protect against a loss greater than 25 percent.

The covered call strategy does not provide significant downside protection. The downside protection provided is equal to the value of the call option sold. This value received for the option is called the premium. A simple example may help in the understanding of this strategy. Let's assume an investor owns shares in the retailer, Kohl's. The price of Kohl's stock (when I wrote this section of the book) was $74. You decide that, based on your analysis, the stock is trading at a high level, and you do not care if part of your stock gets called away at a price just marginally higher than the current price. You sell a call at $80 that expires five months from now. The investor receives a premium (payment) of $2.90 for each share as the price of the call.

If the stock does not reach $80, the investor who sold the call gets to keep the stock and essentially pockets an extra $2.90 for every share. This provides the investor an extra 3.9 percent return on his or her Kohl's stock. If the stock does get called at $80, the investor will have to sell the stock at $80 per share and, combined with the $2.90 premium, he or she will effectively cash out of his or her stock at $82.90 per share. This provides the investor a return of 11.5 percent over the current price of the stock and in the five-month timeframe of the call option.

Healthy Investment Tips

1. Pay attention to potential risks; they come in many forms that investors need to be aware of and understand.
2. Know what types of risk control and risk-reducing strategies you can employ in your portfolio.
3. Understand risks beyond volatility.

19

Everybody Has His or Her Own Style: Should Investors Have Their Own Style, Too?

Style: *A way in which something is done, processed, or performed*

Every individual has his or her own unique style. In the investment world, the same thing holds true. Many investment managers, investment firms, and advisors have their own defined style of investing. The investment profession has attempted to neatly categorize different investment managers, investment firms, mutual funds, and, in some cases, advisors into style boxes, so to speak. Presumably, the reason for this is so that investors can more easily evaluate who is a good and skilled manager—and who is not.

MOST COMMON STYLE CATEGORIES

1. **Growth:** This style usually describes investment managers who look for stocks that are growing their revenue and earnings at faster rates than others in the industry. These companies often set very high bars for themselves, which causes them to be aggressive in expanding their business through geographic reach, market share expansion, new product development, and acquisition.

2. **Value:** This style usually describes investment managers who look for stocks that are cheap on some basis relative to others in the market and industry. The typical measures used by value managers to ascertain whether a company is cheap include price-to-book value, price to earnings, free-cash flow, and price-to-sales.

3. **Growth at a Reasonable Price (GARP):** This style is usually dominated with growth characteristics and an eye toward value. GARP managers often pay close attention to what is called the price/earnings to growth (PEG) ratio. The PEG ratio is simply the price of the stock divided by its earnings growth. GARP managers want growth companies, but not growth at any price.

4. **Contrarian:** These are the so-called plaid pants investment managers who go against the mainstream consensus view. These managers often buy what no one else wants. They look for stocks and industries that are out of favor and unloved by other investors. The viewpoint of these managers is that contrarian stocks are beaten down more than justified. In many cases, companies that fall into the contrarian camp are making progress to turn themselves around, but are given little credit for their efforts by investors.

Investment styles go in and out of favor, so it is a good idea to be exposed to more than one style in your portfolio. It is difficult to predict style turning points, but as a rule of thumb, they last anywhere from three to six years. Figure 52 shows the seven style cycles that have occurred between growth and value since 1979.

In the bond world, styles are described somewhat differently than in the stock market. Bond managers are usually lumped into the following categories:

1. **Total Return:** This means that the manager is looking not just for income, but appreciation as well. What this usually means is that the bond manager must make a bet on interest rate movements and be on the right side of that bet in order to get appreciation. In lower quality circles, appreciation potential can come from other sources, such as spread narrowing, quality upgrades, restructuring, and so forth.

Figure 52   Historical Style Cycles

Russell 1000®

Style Cycle	Annualized Returns			Cumulative Returns		
	Russell 1000® Growth	Russell 1000® Value	Difference	Russell 1000® Growth	Russell 1000® Value	Difference
01/79-06/83	20.12	19.68	0.45	128.22	124.41	3.81
07/83-09/88	9.67	16.12	-6.45	62.37	119.16	-56.79
10/88-12/91	23.17	12.49	10.68	96.85	46.60	50.25
01/91-12/97	16.07	20.08	-4.01	144.47	199.76	-55.29
01/98-06/00	29.95	7.16	22.79	92.52	18.87	73.65
07/00-02/09	-9.87	-1.82	-8.05	-59.02	-14.60	-44.42
03/09-06/11	34.36	33.31	1.05	94.35	90.97	3.37

Russell 2000®

Style Cycle	Annualized Returns			Cumulative Returns		
	Russell 2000® Growth	Russell 2000® Value	Difference	Russell 2000® Growth	Russell 2000® Value	Difference
01/79-06/83	33.23	31.81	1.42	263.70	246.53	17.18
07/83-09/88	0.45	10.54	-10.09	2.50	73.50	-71.00
10/88-12/91	14.48	7.61	6.87	50.05	24.62	25.42
01/91-12/97	11.90	21.18	-9.28	96.29	216.68	-120.39
01/98-06/00	22.64	-1.94	24.59	58.30	-4.32	62.62
07/00-02/09	-7.13	2.92	-10.05	-47.01	28.03	-75.04
03/09-06/11	44.12	39.37	4.75	127.59	111.06	16.53

(January 1979 through June 2011)
Note: Indexes are unmanaged and cannot be invested in directly. Past performance is not indicative of future results.

Data Source: Dennis J. Tritton, *Russell Research: Has Growth Become Value*, "Historical Style Cycles – Value versus Growth in Russell 1000® and Russell 2000®", March 2007.
Data Source: Morningstar, Inc.

2. **Sector Spread:** This is where a manager will overweight or underweight various sectors of the bond market based on the interest rate spread between sectors.

3. **Buy and Hold:** This is where a manager puts together a bond portfolio and typically does not trade it. The manager's job in this case mainly revolves around replacing maturities or bonds that are called. Often, managers using a buy-and-hold strategy will purchase what is referred to as a "bond ladder." A bond ladder is simply a portfolio of individual bonds that have staggered maturity dates such that the investor has a bond maturing every year over a several-year timeframe.

4. **High Yield:** In this style category, a bond manger invests in bonds that are rated below investment grade. This carries substantially more risk in the form of defaults, the price that investors are willing to pay relative to investment grade bonds, and the marketability of the bonds if there is a need to sell for various reasons.

5. **Passive:** This category is made up of managers who try to replicate some bond index and then provide performance as close to that index as possible. There are numerous bond indices that managers track and the investor needs to understand the differences in maturities, credit quality, and types of bonds that each index holds, and then determine the suitability of each relative to their own situation.

Healthy Investment Tips

1. Investment styles go in and out of favor. Make sure you are diversified by style; don't fall in love with just one style and have your portfolio completely devoted to that.
2. Be careful to not attribute investment performance that may simply be due to style cycles to the manager doing either a good or bad job.

20

How Do You Know You Need a Hip Replacement? Or, When to Sell, When to Buy, and When to Do Nothing?

Hip Replacement: Used to repair joint failure and to relieve pain and improve function

In Chapter 5, I discussed the dangers of putting too much emphasis on past investment performance. Yet, there must be a time to bail out of the market or a time when you should bail out of individual managers or individual stocks. Is this right or wrong? Read on to learn the answer.

TOTAL MARKET BAILOUT

First, let's address the issue of bailing out of the market. I would never advise wholesale bailing out of the market. If you want good evidence of the danger of this, look at Figure 53, a table on the impact on performance of missing the best ten months during various multi-year periods of the market.

This table shows the value of $1,000 invested in the S&P 500 Index during various time periods. The results show the value if the money was untouched, if it was not in the market for the top ten performing months, and if it missed the top twenty performing months.

Figure 53   Missing the Best Ten Months in the Market

	1972-2010	1991-2010	2001-2010
Untouched	$ 41,679	$ 5,751	$ 1,151
Missing 10 Top-Performing Months	$ 13,215	$ 2,445	$ 528
Missing 20 Top-Performing Months	$ 5,697	$ 1,245	$ 315

The problem is that your timing of when to get out the market and when to get back into the market has to be *extremely* lucky in order to add any value to your portfolio. The greater likelihood, which the data bears out, is that you will hurt your overall performance by wholesale market timing moves. Missing just the best ten months over the last ten years would have cut your returns by more than 50 percent. Missing the best twenty months over the last ten years would have cut your returns by more than 70 percent!

In the following paragraphs, I will cover "red flags," or indicators of when to exit a stock, ideas on when to buy (and techniques for doing so), some thoughts on information versus noise, and a few tips on what to buy.

RED FLAGS

Figuring out when to sell an investment can be very difficult. This is challenging even for investment professionals who make it their full-time jobs to manage money. As a result of this problem, many professionals establish rules that if the price of a stock is down by more than a set percentage, they sell. The stop-loss, as this is referred to, is often set at 15, 20, or 25 percent drops in the stock price. The theory behind this is that the market knows something they do not, and they should pay attention to that information.

The problem with the stop-loss theory is that the market often overreacts to bad news, and selling on that news will frequently get you out at a price worse than what is justified. Often, that price will turn out to be the bottom, not really saving you from a loss, but simply locking in that loss. A better approach may be to look for qualitative reasons to hit the exits.

If you want to follow a qualitative approach to determining when to exit a stock, these red flags may be useful:

1. **You have spotted a rat.** Growing up on the farm, I knew that if I saw one rat, there were others lurking nearby. Some investors believe this is true with companies. Whether the rat is a piece of bad news or a manager who does something unethical, the belief is that there is more where that came from. Spotting a rat could be a reason to sell.

2. **The company never reinvents itself.** This can especially be a problem for a technology or consumer product company that has great success for several years due to popular products, but then does not adapt to the changing needs and preferences of the consumer. There are always examples of these types of companies in any market environment.

3. **Many excuses.** The company blames external factors for its problems. Sometimes these are legitimate, but look for a pattern of excuses.

4. **Key departures.** The company loses a key executive, like the CFO or CEO, and the explanation is sketchy. This can be a red flag that some problem has been uncovered, but not yet communicated to investors.

5. **The company unexpectedly replaces its auditor.** To follow my anatomy theme, this could be like firing your doctor because you didn't like the prognosis. The replacement of an auditor can easily be a non-issue, but it has been a red flag often enough that it is worth paying attention to.

WHEN TO BUY

When it seems like everything in the media is negative on the market, you should consider buying. When the next piece of bad news has little impact on the market, there is a good chance you are getting close to the bottom of the market. The problem is you won't feel like buying. This is why the notion of the shopping list that I discussed in Chapter 9 is important. Have that list developed with some names of investments and the price levels at which you would be a buyer.

The techniques for buying by individual investors include dividend reinvestment plans (DRIPs), dollar-cost averaging, and buying the dips. The first two techniques are largely automatic, which means that you are not going to try and find the best time to buy, but you are going to buy a little all the time.

Many companies allow you to buy as little as one share of stock and then enroll in their DRIPs. Not only can you reinvest the dividends and get more stock with that reinvestment, you can also add money for additional purchases of the stock—typically, on a monthly or quarterly basis.

DRIPs can be a great way to accumulate stock when you have a relatively small amount of money to invest—usually significantly less than the minimums required for mutual funds. The advantages of DRIPs are that they can be a fun way for people to start investing with minimal initial dollars to invest. Over time, if you stick with it, you could accumulate a decent-sized portfolio. This is how I established some initial positions in some selected stocks a number of years ago. The disadvantages are primarily related to diversification issues—it will be difficult to get diversified across enough names—and tracking taxes on all those separate purchases of stock that could complicate your tax filing if you sell the stock down the road.

Dollar-cost averaging is another common buying technique. This is simply putting your plan on automatic pilot by investing a set amount of money periodically, usually either every month or every week. This has the advantage of forcing a degree of discipline in the investing of some of your current income, and buying more shares when stocks are low and less shares when stocks are high.

Buy on the dips is a favorite strategy of investors who believe that stocks will go up over time and that you should buy on sale, as I also discussed in Chapter 9. This strategy helps you avoid buying stocks at their highest prices. However, just because you buy on the dip does not mean the market could not dip further. This strategy also does not provide any assurance that you will buy at anywhere close to the lowest prices, just not at the highest prices.

Look for corrections as market entry points. See Figure 54 for the average frequency of 5 percent and 10 percent corrections.

WHEN IS INFORMATION JUST NOISE THAT YOU SHOULD IGNORE?

It is difficult to answer this question with any degree of certainty. There are times when the market gets overly excited about a group of stocks, and valuations move up quickly on the excitement. We have seen this with telecom stocks, Internet stocks, alternative energy stocks, and in areas such as biotech and nanotech. As of this writing, social networking companies have com-

Figure 54   A History of Declines: 1900 to December 2010

A history of declines (1900–December 2010)

Type of decline	Average frequency of decline	Average length of decline	Last occurrence	Previous occurrence
–5% or more	About 3 times a year	47 days	August 2010	July 2010
–10% or more	About once a year	115 days	July 2010	March 2009
–15% or more	About once every 2 years	217 days	March 2009	March 2008
–20% or more	About once every 3 ½ years	338 days	March 2009	October 2002

Past results are not predictive of results in future periods.

Source: Capital Research and Management Company[SR]

[1] Assumes 50% recovery rate of lost value.

[2] Measures market high to market low.

manded the attention of investors. Valuations of stocks in areas that are highly favored by investors can get ahead of fundamentals and long-term growth potential.

Investors willing to take above-average risk for above-average return potential may consider a portion of their portfolios for these sectors of the market. However, they should be very careful not to get too caught up in the euphoria. Being well-diversified across many economic sectors and industries may help to mitigate the risk of investing in areas of the market that are in favor as well as areas of the market that are out of favor.

HOW TO KNOW WHAT FUNDS OR MANAGERS TO BUY?

First, whatever you buy should fit within your overall portfolio asset allocation plan. Second, you should focus your manager selection on the asset classes where you have a reasonable chance to add the most excess return. Third, when picking active managers, make sure you put at least as much emphasis on the qualitative factors as the quantitative factors.

The following qualitative factors can be used as a guide to help in picking managers:

1. **Consistency of investment process.** Does the manager stick with his or her process rather than flip-flop around?

2. **Experience of key investment personnel.** Have the key decision-makers experienced multiple market cycles managing this investment process?

3. **Stability of key personnel.** Has the key investment team stayed together for at least the last five years?

4. **Adequate resources.** Does the firm have the resources to provide sufficient research, support, client service, technology, and backup?

Healthy Investment Tips

1. Do not attempt to time the market. Returns tend to come in bunches, and being out of the market (for even a short period of time) could mean substantial opportunity lost.
2. When looking at companies or managers, pay attention to "red flags."
3. Look for corrections as potential market entry points.

21

Next Steps: The Checklist

Checklist: A list of tasks in a format designed to aid memory

Up until this point, we have covered a lot of information on the anatomy and have attempted to make connections to investment concepts and ideas that I believe are important. Now what? Well, I have put together this simple checklist to help you move forward with your investment journey:

1. ❑ Take inventory of where you are today.
2. ❑ Prepare a simple balance sheet like the one here in Chapter 21.
3. ❑ Once you have completed the inventory of your assets, liabilities, and cash flow, work on developing your goals (see Chapter 2). After you do this, write them down in an investment policy statement (see Chapter 4).
4. ❑ At this point you may also have some adjustments to make in your financial life based on your balance sheet and cash flow statement. For example, if your cash outflow is greater than your cash inflow, then you may, at a minimum, need to engage in some financial triage to bring your spending back in alignment. If left unchecked, the negative cash flow will impact your balance sheet—and not in a positive way.
5. ❑ The next step is to decide if you want to try to do this yourself, or if you want to go ahead and hire an advisor. You may even want to move this step higher on the list—right after you determine your goals—so that if

you do decide to hire an advisor, the advisor can help in the creation of the investment policy statement.

6. ❏ Use the list of self-discovery questions in Chapter 15 to help get a clear understanding of how you want to proceed as an investor and assess what role you want an advisor to play (if you choose that option). This chapter also provides helpful guidance on choosing the right advisor for you and your situation.

7. ❏ The next step is to decide on how best to fill in your asset allocation. You should have already determined the overall asset allocation decision by this point, but now you need to decide what to buy in each asset class.

8. ❏ Review Chapter 12 to determine the appropriate investment vehicles to use in constructing your portfolio.

9. ❏ Consult with your advisor or do your own due diligence to decide on specific investment options.

10. ❏ Remember to be diversified within each asset class to improve your probability of long-term investment success.

11. ❏ Whether you hire an advisor or move toward your investment goals alone, commit to a regular portfolio review (see Chapter 13 for items to cover during the review).

12. ❏ Monitor your asset allocation. Look for opportunities throughout the year to rebalance and harvest losses, as appropriate (Chapter 11).

13. ❏ Filter out the noise and avoid the temptation to attempt the timing of the market or to flip-flop managers who are not bad, just out of favor or out of style at the moment (Chapters 6 and 19).

14. ❏ Consider risk control strategies to help protect your portfolio and your peace of mind (Chapter 18).

Figure 55   Personal Financial Worksheet

Assets	
Cash	
Savings Account(s)	
Checking Account(s)	
Term Account(s) – CD's, etc.	
Retirement Plans	
Securities, Stocks & Bonds	
Mutual Funds	
Annuities	
Real Estate	
Automobiles/Boats	
Other Valuable Personal Property/Assets	
	Total Assets:
Liabilities	
Home Mortgage	
Other Real Estate Loans	
Automobile Loans	
Bank Loans	
Personal Loans	
Charge Account Debt	
Other Debts	
	Total Liabilities:
Net Worth	
Total Assets	
Minus Total Liabilities	
	Total Net Worth:

Source: Author Analysis

Figure 56 Monthly Cash Flow Statement

Monthly Income Source	Your Income	Spouse/ Partner	Income Total
Salary/wages from employment			
Salary from self-employment			
Social Security benefit			
Pension benefit			
IRA income (distribution)			
Alimony			
Rental property income			
Investment Income (if same every month)			
Inheritance/Trust			
Gifts			
Other income			
Total Monthly Income			

Monthly Expense Category	Your Expenses	Spouse/ Partner	Expense Total
Insurance			
Dental, Medical			
Automobile			
Disability, Long-term care			
Telecom / Internet			
Education			
Federal income tax			
State income tax			
Property tax			
Housing/Rent			
Food			
Utilities			
Home maintenance & improvements			
Travel – vacations			
Charitable donations			
Transportation			
Entertainment			
Personal			
Other expenses			
Total Monthly Expense			

Source: Author Analysis

22

Summary of Healthy Investment Tips

In this final chapter, I will summarize the key takeaways discussed within this book. I will categorize these by topic to provide you with an easy summary of what I believe are important considerations as you move forward on your investing journey.

PREPARATION

- Separate your savings from your investments.
- Live below your means to create financial margin in your life.
- Increased life expectancy and the length of retirement is cause to evaluate or review retirement asset allocations.
- *Never* take money out of your investment accounts prior to retirement.
- Identify your investment goals.
- Develop an investment plan and then document that plan in your investment policy statement.
- Don't start selecting investment vehicles for your portfolio until the asset allocation decision is made.
- When you do start selecting investment vehicles for your portfolio, make sure you understand the pros and cons of each and how they fit into your portfolio.

BALANCE IN YOUR LIFE

- The asset allocation decision is the most important decision an investor can make.
- Structure your portfolio with a core that can provide a steady flow of dividends and income.
- Structure your portfolio for a smooth ride.
- There is a role for both active and passive investment approaches within most investors' portfolios.
- Average in, rebalance out as an effective way to manage risk in your portfolio.

THE POSITIVE CHOICES

- Plan some fun, creativity, and learning into your investment journey.
- Exercise patience and discipline in sticking with your investment plan.
- Look forward, not backward.
- Investing with the heart can mean applying some SRI principles.
- Review your portfolio regularly—schedule and plan it!
- Patient investors can often generate returns by finding contrarian investments.
- The economic cycles can provide you with opportunities.
- Develop a shopping list and strive to buy on sale.
- Develop an illiquidity target weighting for your portfolio, and then let your required asset allocation be a guide in directing you to the right types of fewer liquid investments.

THE POOR CHOICES

- Avoid extremes of fear and greed.
- Mental accounting can be a useful way to think about your portfolio and avoid emotional decisions.
- Take drawdown risk into consideration when structuring your portfolio.

- Turn off information overload.
- If it doesn't pass the smell test, or if it sounds too good to be true, avoid it.
- The more your assets are scattered with various investment providers, the harder it will be to manage your asset allocation.
- Concentrations are a big risk to your portfolio.
- Investors who fail to diversify their assets globally may miss out on important opportunities.
- Understand the amount of leverage being used in your portfolio.
- Remember that we have a natural bias to react more to negative information than to positive information. Be careful in reacting too strongly to negative information.

GETTING HELP

- Figure out what you want an advisor to do for you before starting the selection process.
- Thoroughly research the background, credentials, experience, and regulatory record of any potential advisor.
- If information overload is a problem, use an experienced advisor to help you stay on track and manage the flow of information you receive.
- Understand the advisor's investment philosophy and process, and make sure it is a good match with your own beliefs.

HOW ARE YOU DOING?

- Utilize an appropriate performance benchmark that is helpful to you in measuring how you are doing relative to your investment goals.
- Monte Carlo analysis can help you determine the probability of meeting your investment goals.
- Tax-efficient investing and harvesting losses can contribute significantly to your after-tax investment returns.

- There may be advantages in placing certain types of investments in tax-deferred accounts and other types in taxable accounts to take advantage of their unique tax characteristics.
- If you own bonds in your portfolio, periodically do the math to determine if you are better off using taxable or tax-exempt bonds.
- Have at least a five-year time horizon, and preferably ten years, when investing in stocks.

One of the important points I want to leave you with is this: **There are no shortcuts as you develop and implement a successful investment strategy.** Just as in caring for your body, a lot of hard work and discipline are required to keep your portfolio healthy. This is not always a popular message in a world impacted by instant gratification, but it is a message that, if followed, will improve your chances of investment success, improve the likelihood of meeting your goals, and leave you less anxious about your future.

Appendix I

Life Stages Investing

An important aspect of the anatomy of investing is considering how your investment plan changes as you go through life and experience changes, including getting older. In this section, I will go through several categories of life stages and some key investment considerations for each of these stages.

TODDLER TO TEN

During this age category—from birth to ten years of age—the considerations laid out are guideposts for parents and grandparents as they initiate the first investments for a child. Several things are important to think about at this stage. The first is the value of compounding and the long-term investment timeframe. At this age, the young investor can benefit the most from a long expected lifespan. Going for growth makes a lot of sense here. It makes little sense to invest conservatively in money markets or bonds.

A portfolio that is oriented toward growth, investing in international and domestic stocks, real estate, and commodities may be appropriate. Figure 57 shows a potential mix of investments and different percentage allocations that you could use as an initial starting point to consider.

The second key consideration at this stage is diversification. Often the young investor gets a modest amount of money, and there is a temptation to buy one or two good stocks. However, the risk of picking the wrong ones is potentially high and could partially or completely offset the long-time horizon principle. The way to circumvent this is to invest in diversified mutual funds or ETFs that give exposure to the asset classes listed in the preceding pie chart. This gives the

Figure 57   Sample Investment Allocation

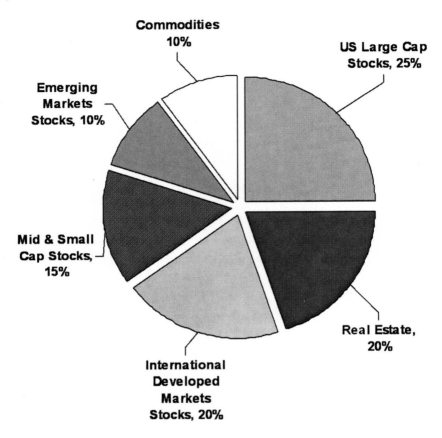

Source: Author Analysis

young investor the opportunity to participate in the upward bias of the market over time without worrying about specific stock risk.

If you are a grandparent, rather than buy a savings bond with a low-interest rate, ask the parents if they have any mutual funds to which you could contribute for the child. (Again, this will likely result in a much higher growth of principal over time than the savings bond.)

Allowances on a weekly basis are often started during this age category. Many parents start allowances when the child starts school. This weekly allowance should be modest to teach the child the basics of money. I have often seen the allowance in dollars equal the age of the child at this stage.

TEN TO TEEN

This is where you can start to go beyond the basics. An important element in this age category is to help the child learn the value of money. How much money does it take to buy an iPod or a cell phone? How much does it cost per month to download songs for your iPod or pay for a calling plan that includes enough text messaging, Wi-Fi, various apps, etc.? The parent should include the child in these discussions and decisions so the child understands that there is a one-time cost and an ongoing cost of owning things. Ideally, the child should have to pay for a portion of these costs either out of his or her allowance or spending budget.

The principle of delayed gratification is important to instill at this age. Waiting and saving for purchases now is good training for later in life. If children in this age bracket are not taught about waiting, they will likely have a difficult time saving and investing in the future. The notion of saving for specific purchases is a good way to teach delayed gratification. My son saved for months to be able to purchase a drum set. He learned two important lessons during this process. The first is that he needed to make choices about what else he would buy (or not) during the process of saving for the drum set. If he had decided to purchase some new games for his Xbox, he would have had to wait longer to have enough money to buy the drums. The second lesson my son learned was that $500 is a lot of money. Sure, Mom or Dad could have written a check when he first brought up the idea of the drum set and started to petition us for it, but he would not have learned about the value of money had we caved in to that request.

This issue of not learning about delayed gratification surfaces later in life. It surfaces when young workers have difficulty investing enough to get the company match on their 401(k) contributions. They often do not get the full match because of all the stuff they think they need in their lives immediately when they get that first job. This limits their ability to set aside money from their paychecks for retirement.

As the ten-year-old gets to the teen years, a monthly budget can be an effective way to teach practical money management principles. A budget can teach children how to live within boundaries and make responsible choices. A month is a long time for teenagers, and it teaches them to plan ahead—an important element of investing. It also gives them an important taste of the real world, which will help to prepare them for the time when they enter it.

This is also the time to open a checking account and have the teen get a debit card with online access. This allows the teen to start tracking his or her own money and spending habits. Initially, the teen will probably be surprised at how fast the balance shrinks. A precursor to a checking account can be a prepaid debit card. This is a card where you can store any value you want on it, and then let the teen decide how to spend the money, without incurring debt on a credit card.

To encourage saving some of that monthly budget in my own children, I used a matching bonus strategy. If a certain dollar amount was saved from the budget each month, I would match that at the end of the month. I found this to be highly effective for my teenage daughter who would stay home and not go out with friends for a couple of nights if that's what it took in order to not lose that match.

DRIVER TO DIPLOMA

Once a teenager gets a driver's license, the sense of independence ratchets up several notches. He or she is no longer totally dependent on Mom or Dad to take him or her everywhere. This is the age when many teens get their first jobs and, as a result, their income usually increases. Working with the teen to have a budget and a logical spending, saving, and investing plan makes good sense at this stage. Having more income, but no plan on how that gets spent, can create bad habits early in life that will be difficult to correct down the road.

Helping the teen figure out the cost of living is important. Oftentimes, teens are sheltered because the parents pay for most of the living expenses. They have a distorted view of how much money it takes to live. Most of their income is viewed as purely discretionary in their eyes. One successful way I found to help teach my teen about the cost of living was to send my daughter out to the grocery store with a shopping list for the family. I estimated the amount of money the groceries would cost and then transferred that amount of money into my daughter's account. Another useful exercise is to have your teen help pay bills via check or through electronic means. In either case, teens can get a sense of how much things cost and how much it *really* costs to maintain a household.

Using technology tools that appeal to the tech-savvy teenager can also make learning about money management, budgeting, saving, and investing more interesting for a teen. Having your teen's bank accounts online and utilizing Web-based tools are good first steps.

DIPLOMA TO DEGREE

Keeping debt under control is critical at this age. Many college students make decisions during their four or five years of college that will impact them for ten to twelve years after college. Some of these decisions can impede their ability to save and invest during the time of their lives when their expenses should be low and when time is on their side.

Encourage your college student to limit credit card use; have your college student use a debit card instead. It is too easy for teens who are away from home and have newfound freedom to make poor decisions about the use of credit. If they want to use plastic, they should use debit cards that tap money they already have rather than spend money they do not have.

College students who are away from home for the first time need to have a clear understanding with their parents on what expenses they will cover. If the parent is covering tuition, does that mean room, board, and tuition, or does it mean room, board, tuition, books, eating out, gas money, and other entertainment expenses? A good idea for the college student is to have a very detailed budget that covers the essentials of college life. If a parent is helping out, it may make sense to have a quarterly meeting to go over how the budget is working. This may also help in holding the student accountable.

THE FIRST JOB

Welcome to the real world! These next sections will focus on you as the financial decision-maker for your life, not your parents or guardians. Once you land your first job, you should study your company benefits plan. Consult your human resources or benefits department, or ask some co-workers about the different benefits available to you. This will be your first exposure to valuable benefits the company may provide to you free of charge or at a substantially reduced rate. Do not make the mistake of thinking you don't need any benefits. Make sure you get enrolled in a health care plan right away. You were probably carried on your parents' plan while in college, but now you will probably want to get your own health care coverage.

Think long and hard before buying a house. Rent seems like throwing money away, but owning a house can be very expensive and can impact your ability to start a wise investing strategy. If you do purchase a house, make sure it is one with exceptional resale qualities. Your first job will likely not be your last job. You may give yourself a lot more career flexibility for your next position if you do not own a house that you have to unload in order to accept a new opportunity.

The following list offers tips for college students entering the full-time workforce for the first time:

1. Live below your means. Live like a college student the first two or three years after you get your first job, and you will be amazed at how much you can save and invest.

2. Set money aside for emergencies. Set up a separate bank account for this. Try to accumulate enough to cover three to six months of basic living expenses. It will be much easier to do this now than any other time in your life.

3. Start retirement savings with your first paycheck. Most companies offer 401(k) plans that offer some level of matching contributions. This is free money; at a minimum, you want to capture all of that.

4. Create separate savings accounts for large purchases. Never, *ever* withdraw money from an investment account for a purchase of a consumer product.

5. Keep credit card balances low in relation to overall credit availability and your ability to pay it off in full.

6. Avoid the temptation to make spontaneous purchases. Research and comparison-shopping help guard against impulsive moves at the checkout counter. Do a lot of window-shopping, and ask a lot of questions before making any big-ticket purchases. This will delay you actually spending the money and, as time passes, you may even realize that you do not need the product or are not as interested in spending your hard-earned money on it.

7. Borrow prudently. Take out a loan only for purchases that will likely appreciate over time. Avoid borrowing for items such as clothes or furniture, which lose value before the first payment is made.

8. Be a smart car shopper. Consider the resale value of the car before buying. Avoid buying a new car that depreciates the moment you drive it off the lot. Buying a car that is a year or two old with low miles and lots of warranty coverage left can attain a much better value.

9. Learn to enjoy reading. You won't be bored and feel compelled to shop, and you might just learn something in the process.

10. Reward yourself with one modest purchase. Getting that first full-time job is cause for celebration. Treat yourself; just don't go overboard.

11. Invest broadly. Beginning investors have a tendency to pick one stock—often a speculative one—and then get disillusioned with investing if the price falls. That one bad experience can color a person's view of investing for many years. Investing broadly spreads out the risk of making a bad investment pick and increases your chances of a successful experience.

12. Consider hiring a planner to put together a basic financial plan that can become your financial road map for the next several years.

FROM TWENTY-FIVE TO THIRTY-FIVE

During this age range, you are probably doing a number of things: moving up the career ladder, adding credentials or degrees to your resume, getting married, buying a house, starting a family, changing employers, having children, going from one income to two incomes (and then, perhaps, back to one income), moving out of a starter house into a larger house, etc.

With all of these changes come important decisions about your money and how you invest. Mistakes made in this stage can cost you hundreds of thousands of dollars over time. The single most important action item at this stage of life is to prepare a basic financial plan. The basic financial plan can act as a road map for how you spend, how you budget, how you invest, how much debt to take on, how to meet your goals, etc. Engaging a financial planner early on will help you to make informed decisions during this critical life stage.

Figure 58   Major Life Events: Money Tips

Event	Money Tips
Buying Your First House	Buy something you can easily afford to sell when you want to upgrade. Do not buy a bigger house than you can comfortably afford. No more than 30% of your income should go to housing-related costs. Buying the biggest house you can just barely afford is a pitch used by some realtors – ignore it. Buying a house too substantial for your income will not provide you any margin in your financial life.
Getting Married	Be reasonable on how much you spend. According to recent data, the average wedding now costs $27,000! You can have a memorable and quality wedding without spending that much. You don't need to one-up your friends and get too extravagant. That will only add stress to a new marriage as you pay off those bills.
First Child	Make sure you each have enough life insurance to provide for the child for several years if you die unexpectedly. Also, set up a revocable trust that names guardianship of the child and who will manage the assets for the child until they reach an age to manage them themselves.
Getting Promoted	Increase your savings and investments by at least half of your increased level of income. In other words, don't adjust your lifestyle to the new salary level. Adjust your saving and investing instead.
Changing Jobs	Make sure you roll over your 401-k. Understand your new firm benefits package to make full use of it.

Source: Author Analysis

FROM THIRTY-SIX TO FIFTY

This will likely be a period of time when you will enjoy some of your peak earnings years. It will also likely be a time when your family living expenses will be very high as your children get more involved with activities that cost money. You may also be setting aside money for college at the same time that you are paying private school tuition, etc.

Your investment portfolio during these years has hopefully grown to the point where you can do more things with it. You may be able to invest in asset classes that you were not previously able to. You may have enough assets to consider hiring a professional money manager to take your collection of investments and invest on your behalf.

If you self-direct your investments, you may be in a position to start acquiring individual bonds instead of bond funds, separate account managers instead of only mutual funds, and private placements investing in areas such as private real estate or private equity. In most cases, your investment portfolio should continue to be heavily weighted toward asset classes that can provide long-term appreciation for you.

Since these are your peak earnings years, and you have likely accumulated a significant amount of assets during this life stage, you should also think about risk protection to cover both. In other words, you should protect your ability to create an income stream by making sure you have appropriate long-term disability insurance that provides you and your family a stream of income should you become disabled. In addition, and thanks to the fact that we live in a litigious society, you should also make sure you have adequate liability insurance to protect your accumulated assets in the event you are sued.

FROM FIFTY-ONE TO RETIREMENT

From an investment standpoint, this may be your last chance to accumulate assets that will help you for the rest of your life. A number of critical decisions will decide how well you can afford to live in retirement. Some of the issues that you will need to address include: *When should I retire? How much is enough? Do I need to change my asset allocation? Is my portfolio positioned to provide an income stream that will keep up with inflation? What will my other sources of income be?*

It is important to keep your portfolio geared toward growth and not get too conservative going into retirement. Additionally, you may want to start evaluating the cost of your retirement at this point. Trying to figure that out when you were twenty-five probably didn't matter much back then. But now you *need* to think about it. There are some significant differences in costs of living across the country that could make a big difference on how much you will need.

Once you have completed some analysis on your personal cost of retirement, you will want to compare that to what resources you have now and anticipate having when you retire. You may find out that it would be beneficial to delay your retirement for a couple of years or more to build a larger nest egg. Your company may also have some enhanced benefits that you would be eligible for if you work additional years. There may also be an opportunity to transition into retirement by going from full-time to part-time or even reduced time for two or three years to help ease the transition both financially and emotionally. This may also appeal to your company as it allows the company to retain an experienced worker while training a new employee.

This is the stage of life where you may see an early retirement buyout offer from your company. At first, these offers can sound very appealing, and in certain instances, they may very well be. Make sure, however, that you analyze the offer carefully and consider your other options, including the option of not taking the offer or taking the offer and going to work for another company.

RETIREMENT AND BEYOND

One of the first things you need to do, if you have not done so already, is to get your estate plan and will in order. Do this while you are still working if you can to take advantage of any services your company may have to offer. Many companies offer pre-retirement seminars that can provide you with a list of helpful resources and issues to consider. Make sure you also think about the best way to maximize your pension, Social Security, and health care benefits.

Avoid getting too conservative because the retirement years may last twenty-five years or even longer. Purchasing power erosion is a key risk at this stage of life. With just annualized inflation of 3 percent over a twenty-five-year period, the purchasing power of a $1 million portfolio drops to about $478,000 at the end of that time period. An investor who gets too conservative—placing too much in money market or bonds—will likely feel the bulk of this impact.

Appendix II

Case Studies

STUDY 1: YOUNG PROFESSIONALS, MARRIED, NO CHILDREN, IN THEIR MID-TWENTIES

A young couple is looking for guidance and needs someone to walk them through what to do. The first question that needs to be addressed revolves around the couple's current vital signs, which are as follows:

- Both make approximately $45,000 annually; annual family income is $90,000
- No immediate plan for kids, but a family is wanted someday
- Live in a townhouse and have 5 percent equity in it; also have a mortgage
- Have two cars—one is owned and one is leased; have an outstanding loan on the owned vehicle00
- One spouse still paying off student loans
- Other spouse still paying down credit card bill from wedding expenses

Recommended Action Steps to Consider

These are their top priorities:

- They should take advantage of their 401(k)s and get the full match.
- They should invest in a 401(k) for growth, but be diversified.
- They should start building a six-month cash reserve.

These are their second priorities:

- They should start a savings account for their future needs for the family.
- They should pay a little extra every month on the mortgage.

Example asset allocation for aggregate investment portfolio, including 401(k) and IRA balances, is shown in Figure 59.

Figure 59   Asset Allocation Breakdown: Case 1

Asset Type	Example Allocation (As a % of Total Portfolio)
U.S. Large Cap Stocks	28%
International Stocks	18%
U.S. Mid Cap Stocks	9%
Real Estate	10%
U.S. Small Cap Stocks	8%
Emerging Markets Stocks	7%
Commodities	5%
Emerging Market Bonds	5%
High Yield Bonds	5%
Short/Intermediate Bonds	5%

Source: Author Analysis

STUDY 2: STILL YOUNG PROFESSIONALS, MARRIED, TWO KIDS, IN THEIR MID-30S

Current vital signs regarding the family's financial health:

- One spouse at home with kids; other spouse has annual income of $100,000
- Own a four-bedroom house, 30 percent equity, mortgage, and modest outstanding home equity loan
- Two cars with loans outstanding on both
- No student loans or outstanding credit card balances

- 401(k) and IRA combined balance of $125,000
- Savings account with balance of $2,500

Recommended Action Steps to Consider

- They should take advantage of the 401(k) and get the full match (if they are not already doing so).
- They should start modest payroll contributions to 529 college plans for the two kids.
- They should continue adding to their savings account (through payroll deductions) for emergency needs.
- They should start a taxable brokerage investment account with any windfall, such as a bonus or a tax refund.
- They should make sure their 401(k) is well-diversified and positioned for growth.

Example asset allocation for aggregate investment portfolio, including 401(k) and IRA balances, is shown in Figure 60.

Figure 60 Asset Allocation Breakdown: Case 2

Asset Type	Example Allocation (As a % of Total Portfolio)
U.S. Large Cap Stocks	28%
International Stocks	18%
U.S. Mid Cap Stocks	9%
Real Estate	10%
U.S. Small Cap Stocks	8%
Emerging Markets Stocks	7%
Commodities	5%
Emerging Market Bonds	5%
High Yield Bonds	5%
Short/Intermediate Bonds	5%

Source: Author Analysis

STUDY 3: STILL THINK THEY'RE YOUNG PROFESSIONALS, MARRIED, TWO KIDS, IN THEIR MID-40S

Current vital signs regarding the family's financial health:

- One spouse employed part-time with annual income of $25,000; other spouse has annual income of $110,000
- Own four-bedroom house with 50 percent equity, mortgage, and modest home equity loan outstanding
- Three cars (one child is driver) and two outstanding car loans
- Modest credit card balances outstanding from recent family vacations
- 401(k) and IRA combined balances of $250,000
- Savings account with balance of $1,000

Recommended Action Steps to Consider

- Time is still on their side. They should avoid the temptation to get too conservative with their retirement assets.
- They should rebuild their savings account for an emergency fund.
- They should pay off their credit card balances as quickly as possible.
- They should start a taxable brokerage account with any windfall, such as a bonus or a tax refund.
- They should continue contributions to their 529 plan for their children's college expenses.

Example asset allocation for aggregate investment portfolio, including 401(k) and IRA balances, is shown in Figure 61.

STUDY 4: PROFESSIONALS, EMPTY NESTERS, MID-TO-LATE 50S, WOULD LIKE TO RETIRE IN FIVE TO SEVEN YEARS

Current vital signs regarding the family's financial health:

- Total annual family income of $150,000

Figure 61 Asset Allocation Breakdown: Case 3

Asset Type	Example Allocation (As a % of Total Portfolio)
U.S. Large Cap Stocks	28%
International Stocks	18%
U.S. Mid Cap Stocks	8%
Real Estate	10%
U.S. Small Cap Stocks	8%
Emerging Markets Stocks	7%
Commodities	5%
Emerging Market Bonds	5%
High Yield Bonds	5%
Short/Intermediate Bonds	5%

Source: Author Analysis

- Family residence is paid off; however, modest home equity loan is outstanding
- Have two cars; one with outstanding loan
- Modest outstanding credit card balances (to help with wedding expenses of recently married adult child)
- 401(k) and IRA balances of $500,000
- Taxable brokerage account balance of $200,000
- Savings account balance of $2,500

Recommended Action Steps to Consider

- They should continue to maximize their contributions to their 401(k).
- They should ratchet up their contributions to their taxable brokerage account in order to have enough investments for retirement in five to seven years.
- They should pay off any remaining debt—their credit cards first, then their home equity loan.

- They should build their emergency savings account through payroll deductions.

- They should consider modest asset allocation rebalancing. They may also have enough investment assets to diversify their stock holdings into some absolute return strategies.

- Example asset allocation for aggregate investment portfolio, including 401(k) and IRA balances, is shown in Figure 62.

Figure 62   Asset Allocation Breakdown: Case 4

Asset Type	Example Allocation (As a % of Total Portfolio)
U.S. Large Cap Stocks	28%
International Stocks	18%
U.S. Mid Cap Stocks	9%
Real Estate	10%
Short/Intermediate Bonds	10%
Emerging Markets Stocks	5%
Commodities	5%
Emerging Market Bonds	5%
High Yield Bonds	5%
U.S. Small Cap Stocks	5%

Source: Author Analysis

STUDY 5: RETIRED, MID-TO-LATE 60S

Current vital signs regarding family's financial health:

- Income includes $24,000 from Social Security and $60,000 withdrawal from portfolio on an annual basis

- No mortgage or home equity balance on family home

- Two cars; no loans

- Modest outstanding credit card balance from a recent cruise vacation

- Combined retirement account balance of $1,000,000
- Taxable brokerage account balance of $400,000
- Savings account balance of $5,000

Recommended Action Steps to Consider

- They should keep their spending under control to preserve retirement assets.
- They should consider modest rebalancing of their family portfolio to become a little less aggressive. They may also be able to use some absolute return strategies in place of a portion of their stock holdings.
- They should balance withdrawals from their taxable account with withdrawals from their retirement accounts. They should also keep in mind the tax differences on the distribution and the tax-deferred accumulation of return in the retirement accounts. Furthermore, they should keep in mind upcoming minimum distribution requirements.

Figure 63   Asset Allocation Breakdown: Case 5

Asset Type	Example Allocation (As a % of Total Portfolio)
U.S. Large Cap Stocks	26%
Short/Intermediate Bonds	15%
International Stocks	16%
Real Estate	10%
U.S. Mid Cap Stocks	8%
High Yield Bonds	5%
Commodities	5%
Emerging Market Bonds	5%
Emerging Markets Stocks	5%
U.S. Small Cap Stocks	5%

Source: Author Analysis

Appendix III

Sources of Recommended Online Investor Education and Advisor Information Websites

American Institute of Certified Public Accountants (www.aicpa.org)

Alliance for Investor Education (www.investoreducation.org)

American Association of Individual Investors (www.aaii.com)

American Association of Retired Persons (www.aarp.org/money)

American Financial Services Association Education Foundation (www.afsaef.org)

American Savings Education Council (www.choosetosave.org/asec)

BetterInvesting (formerly known as NAIC) (www.betterinvesting.org)

Certified Financial Planner Board of Standards (www.cfp-board.org)

CFA Institute (www.cfainstitute.org)

Consumer Federation of America (www.consumerfed.org)

Employee Benefit Research Institute (www.ebri.org)

Financial Planning Association (www.fpanet.org)

FINRA, Financial Industry Regulatory Authority (www.finra.org)

Forbes (www.forbes.com)

Foundation for Investor Education (www.pathtoinvesting.org)

Investment Company Institute (www.ici.org)

Investment Management Consultants Association (www.imca.org)

Investor Protection Trust (www.investorprotection.org)

Jump$tart Coalition (www.jumpstart.org)

Museum of American Finance (www.financialhistory.org)

National Academy Foundation (www.naf.org)

National Association of State Treasurers Foundation (www.tomorrows-money.org)

National Center on Education and the Economy (www.ncee.org)

National Endowment for Financial Education (www.nefe.org)

National Foundation for Credit Counseling (www.nfcc.org)

National Futures Association (www.nfa.futures.org)

New York Stock Exchange (www.nyse.com/)

Options Industry Council (www.8880ptions.com)

Public Company Accounting Oversight Board (www.pcaobus.org)

Stock Market Game (www.smgww.org)

Appendix IV

Sample Investment Policy Statement

Investment Policy Statement

This Investment Policy Statement is being prepared for:_____
Federal Tax Rate: _____
State Tax Rate: _____

This document outlines the established objectives, policies, and guidelines for the investment of the portfolio's assets.

Purpose of the Investment Policy Statement

The purpose of this Investment Policy Statement is to establish an understanding as to the investment goals, objectives, and management policies for this portfolio.

The Investment Policy Statement will also:

1. Establish overall standards for the management of the assets held in the portfolio.
2. Define overall investment parameters to help manage risk in the portfolio in accordance with the identified risk tolerance.
3. Communicate the intent of this plan to the appropriate parties.
4. Provide a written strategy and standard, which will guide the decisions regarding the management of the portfolio assets, including any restrictions to the management of the assets.
5. Establish a methodology for evaluating the performance of the portfolio and its components. This statement should be reviewed periodically, and revisions should be made, as necessary, to reflect changes in circumstances or objectives. All revisions must be made in writing and distributed to the appropriate parties on a timely basis.

Investment Objective

The Investor's investment objective is: _____

Example:

Emphasis is on long-term potential capital appreciation with some consideration for current income. Investments are primarily in equity securities and other asset classes with growth as the primary objective. Fixed-income securities are utilized for risk control.

This objective can be considered for investors with above-average risk tolerances for principal volatility and intermediate to longer-term time horizons. Real estate and alternative investments (e.g., hedge funds, private equity, commodities) may be utilized to improve the return/risk relationship of the portfolio. Investor suitability, liquidity needs, investment minimum requirements, and investor qualifications will be considered before investing in these asset classes.

Investment Horizon

The investor has an investment horizon of _____ years. This is the amount of time before all, or a significant portion (at least 50 percent) of, the portfolio's assets would be distributed.

Tax Sensitivity

Investor is aware that any investments made in this account may be subject to U.S. federal or state reporting and/or taxes, including but not limited to income, withholding, generation skipping, gift, or estate tax. Investor should consult with Investor's own legal and tax advisors regarding the types of investments to be made in this account, and regarding all assets transferred into this account to determine the U.S. tax consequences of such investments.

If applicable, and the Investor is a non-resident alien (NRA), assets may be subject to U.S. federal or state reporting and/or taxes depending upon the types of investments.

If applicable, external money managers utilized by the Advisor will manage client assets in accordance with previously disclosed investment styles. The money managers will not alter their investment selections or their investment style to take into consideration the U.S. federal or state tax consequences of such investments to NRA clients, which may result in an account being subject to certain U.S. federal or state taxes (including but not limited to income, capital gains, estate, or gift taxes) and/or reporting.

Risk Tolerance

Historical capital market data, together with modern investment theory, indicate a relationship between the level of risk (volatility) and the level of return that can be expected.

Higher returns are typically associated with higher risk; therefore, the risk profile of the aggregate plan assets should parallel the volatility of the total plan benchmark.

Asset Allocation Strategy

After consideration of the Investor's investment objective, risk tolerance, and other portfolio specifications, the initial allocation will be:

Asset Class	Value	Percent	Range*
Equities	$0	0%	X%–XX%
Fixed-Income	$0	0%	X%–XX%
Real Estate	$0	0%	X%–XX%
Alternative Invest	$0	0%	X%–XX%
Cash Equivalents	$0	0%	
Other	$0	0%	
Unclassified	$0	0%	
Total Assets	$0	100%	

*Ranges may fluctuate and/or change from what is noted due to new asset allocation recommendations. Asset allocation does not assure or guarantee better performance and cannot eliminate the risk of investment losses.

Portfolio rebalancing shall be performed periodically to remain consistent with the established asset allocation.

At a minimum, the Plan's assets, governed by this Investment Policy Statement, shall be reviewed annually, and trading costs shall be considered if cash flow is insufficient to effect the rebalancing. The allocation does not involve market timing and is intended to represent a diversified approach to investing based upon the Investor's investment horizon.

Investment Timing

The Investor has indicated a preference to have the portfolio represented in this plan fully allocated toward the recommended asset allocation within _____ months.

Performance Evaluation or Monitoring

1. Performance of the Portfolio will be monitored, measured, and evaluated over a market cycle.
2. Performance will be measured against appropriate investor goal(s).

Special Considerations

The Investor has indicated a need for special consideration and as such requires separate handling (or should not be included) in the asset allocation shown above.

    a. A potential cash position greater than 15 percent; and/or

    b. An asset concentration position greater than 10 percent. If special considerations should remain, they should not be reallocated to the recommended portfolio.

Restrictions

The following asset classes, securities, and/or sectors will be excluded from this portfolio:

Investment(s) to be restricted or excluded from portfolio:

- [Restrictions 1]
- [Restrictions 2]
- [Restrictions 3]
- [Restrictions 4]
- [Restrictions 5]

Summary of Investor Situation

This is the section of the Investment Policy Statement that could be used to capture Investor conversations, feelings, and individual or family situations.

Signatories

I/We, the investor(s) or the undersigned person(s) delegated with Investment Authority for the assets under this Investment Policy Statement, accept the above description and direction of investment objectives.

By:_____Date:_____
The Investor(s) or Authorized Signature

By:_____Date:_____
The Investor(s) or Authorized Signature (if more than one)

The Advisor acknowledges the Investment Policy Statement as outlined herein and agrees to monitor and/or restructure the objectives of this Investment Policy Statement, as deemed necessary, on an ongoing basis.

By:_____Date:_____
Authorized Signature

Summary Page of Rebalancing Studies

Figure 64   Comparison of Selected Studies of Portfolio Rebalancing Strategy

	Rebalancing Strategy	Were Transaction Costs Addressed?	Were Taxes Addressed?	Was Risk Addressed?	General Issues / Recommendations
Dybvig (2005) Mean-Variance Portfolio Rebalancing with Transaction Costs	TB	Yes	Yes	No	•Finds that using synthetic equity strategies may be better than trading stocks for <10% drift because of reduced transaction costs •Use futures to keep equity exposure within 3% of target allocation
Leland (1996) Optimal Asset Rebalancing in the Presence of Transaction Costs	TB	Yes	Yes	Yes	•Optimal trading band a function of transaction costs, asset volatility, target asset mix and other parameters
Masters (2005) Rebalancing: An Important Tool for Controlling Portfolio Risk	TP	Yes	Yes	Yes	•Must have disciplined strategy as rebalancing can seem emotionally counterintuitive at times •Tracking error quadruples as portfolio drifts twice as far off target
Smith et al. (2004) Optimal Rebalancing Frequency for Bond/ Stock Portfolios	TB	No	No	No	•Tested range of portfolio constructions •Found that the Fed's monetary policy affected the effectiveness of rebalancing •Study looks at returns, not risk
Sun et al. (2004) Optimal Rebalancing Strategy Using Dynamic Programming for Institutional Portfolios	DR	Yes	Yes	Yes	•Periodic rebalancing is unrelated to market behavior •Tolerance-band rebalancing is arbitrary •If transaction costs outweigh expected benefit, no action should be taken •Use certainty equivalents to rebalance only a subset of all assets
Tokat (2006) Portfolio Rebalancing in Theory and Practice	TB	Yes	Yes	Yes	•High asset correlation decreases the need to rebalance •Longer time horizon increases the need to rebalance •Rebalancing should occur by redirecting cash flows

Key:

TB: Tolerance brands around asset allocation target
TP: Specific percent rebalancing trigger
DR: Dynamic risk-adjusted return trigger

Appendix VI
Sample Risk Tolerance Questionnaire

Figure 65   Risk Tolerance Questionnaire

Check the one box that most closely corresponds to your situation, for each of the following five statements:

	Strongly Disagree ←→ Strongly Agree				
1. **Holding Period:** I am willing to maintain my investment position for 10 years or more.	0 ☐	5 ☐	10 ☐	15 ☐	20 ☐
2. **Investment Goal:** I am more interested in growing the value of my portfolio than simply preserving its value.	0 ☐	5 ☐	10 ☐	15 ☐	20 ☐
3. **Risk Sensitivity:** I am willing to bear the investment risk (volatility, "ups and downs") that is characteristic of stocks and bonds.	0 ☐	5 ☐	10 ☐	15 ☐	20 ☐
4. **Liquidity:** Aside from my portfolio, I have adequate liquid assets to meet my major short-term expenses.	0 ☐	5 ☐	10 ☐	15 ☐	20 ☐
5. **Investment Fortitude:** It is not unusual for markets to experience significant declines over both the short- and long-term, as a result of various events. This could result in a $10,000 portfolio declining to $8,000. If the longer-term outlook remains positive, I would maintain my investment and ride out the downward fluctuation.	0 ☐	5 ☐	10 ☐	15 ☐	20 ☐
Total Score:					

Scoring Methodology

Score Range	0-19	20-39	40-59	60-79	80-100
Risk Profile	Conservative	Moderately-Conservative	Moderate	Moderately-Aggressive	Aggressive

Risk Tolerance Categories

Conservative	Moderately-Conservative	Moderate	Moderately-Aggressive	Aggressive
10% Large Cap Stocks 5% Int'l Stocks 5% Small Cap Stocks 80% Fixed Income	25% Large Cap Stocks 5% Int'l Stocks 10% Small Cap Stocks 60% Fixed Income	40% Large Cap Stocks 10% Int'l Stocks 15% Small Cap Stocks 35% Fixed Income	50% Large Cap Stocks 15% Int'l Stocks 15% Small Cap Stocks 20% Fixed Income	60% Large Cap Stocks 20% Int'l Stocks 20% Small Cap Stocks 0% Fixed Income
Conservative investors prefer very little or no risk of loss. They are concerned with safety of principal and a guaranteed or steady return.	Moderately-conservative investors can accept more risk than conservative investors but still require a low probability of loss. Principal safety is a primary concern.	Moderate investors seek a balance between capital appreciation and stability.	Moderately-aggressive investors seek capital appreciation and are willing to accept some short-term losses for potentially higher returns.	Aggressive investors accept substantial market risk and potential loss of principal in pursuit of higher returns.

Note from Author: These are simple stock and bond-only allocations for illustration purposes, to more easily show the potential differences in a portfolio based on investor risk tolerance. In the Case Studies section, I show allocations that include real estate and commodities, as well.

Asset Class Returns by Holding Period

AUTHOR'S NOTES ON THE FOLLOWING CHARTS

This data goes back to 1957 and shows the range of returns over various time periods for different types of accounts. Individual investors can use this data as a guide to return expectations over different time periods. For example, if you think you will only own large company stocks for five years, it is possible that you could have a negative return over that timeframe.

The S&P 500 chart shows the worst rolling five-year return at -6.63 percent. The average return was 10.69 percent and the highest return was 29.63 percent. This also speaks to holding periods and why I believe stock investors should have at least a ten-year investment time horizon.

ASSET CLASS RETURNS BY HOLDING PERIOD

Figure 66   Intermediate Government Bonds

Return by Holding Period	Minimum Return	Average Return	Maximum Return
1 Month	-6.41%	0.56%	11.98%
3 Month	-6.87%	1.70%	19.15%
6 Month	-7.95%	3.42%	22.28%
1 Year	-5.56%	6.95%	32.70%
3 Years	-0.41%	6.74%	18.40%
5 Years	0.75%	6.63%	19.46%
7 Years	0.99%	6.54%	15.51%
10 Years	1.19%	6.45%	13.73%
15 Years	1.38%	6.22%	11.36%
20 Years	1.58%	6.02%	10.50%

Data Source: MorningStar EnCorr, May 2011

Figure 67   The Russell 2000 Index

Return by Holding Period	Minimum Return	Average Return	Maximum Return
1 Month	-30.63%	1.11%	16.51%
3 Month	-35.73%	3.43%	29.73%
6 Month	-46.91%	6.77%	52.68%
1 Year	-42.38%	13.17%	97.52%
3 Years	-17.85%	10.52%	33.93%
5 Years	-6.68%	10.64%	26.69%
7 Years	-1.39%	10.64%	22.64%
10 Years	1.22%	10.38%	17.14%
15 Years	3.97%	10.87%	15.94%
20 Years	6.26%	10.64%	15.14%
25 Years	7.13%	10.52%	13.31%

Data Source: MorningStar EnCorr, May 2011

Figure 68   The Dow Jones: UBS Commodity Index

Return by Holding Period	Minimum Return	Average Return	Maximum Return
1 Month	-21.28%	0.59%	13.00%
3 Month	-35.43%	1.89%	22.45%
6 Month	-49.42%	3.96%	32.37%
1 Year	-50.27%	7.69%	41.56%
3 Years	-11.58%	6.53%	21.83%
5 Years	-3.35%	7.38%	18.60%
7 Years	1.73%	7.31%	15.79%
10 Years	4.09%	7.46%	13.01%
15 Years	5.19%	7.31%	10.79%

Data Source: MorningStar EnCorr, May 2011

Figure 69   The Russell Midcap Index

Return by Holding Period	Minimum Return	Average Return	Maximum Return
1 Month	-24.63%	1.20%	15.37%
3 Month	-38.81%	3.70%	31.40%
6 Month	-46.79%	7.45%	50.51%
1 Year	-46.56%	14.89%	74.60%
3 Years	-17.29%	12.79%	32.26%
5 Years	-5.21%	13.20%	28.58%
7 Years	-0.57%	13.36%	23.56%
10 Years	1.69%	13.16%	20.13%
15 Years	6.31%	13.63%	18.83%
20 Years	8.43%	13.44%	17.86%
25 Years	10.08%	13.26%	15.51%

Data Source: MorningStar EnCorr, May 2011

Figure 70   National Association of Real Estate Investment Trusts (NAREIT) Index

Return by Holding Period	Minimum Return	Average Return	Maximum Return
1 Month	-31.67%	1.10%	31.02%
3 Month	-47.52%	3.34%	39.28%
6 Month	-60.01%	6.86%	71.73%
1 Year	-58.16%	13.99%	106.68%
3 Years	-25.05%	12.82%	33.49%
5 Years	-8.64%	13.67%	29.44%
7 Years	-0.92%	13.87%	23.82%
10 Years	3.43%	13.63%	23.58%
15 Years	4.70%	13.25%	19.19%
20 Years	6.61%	13.10%	16.83%
25 Years	7.83%	13.28%	15.30%
30 Years	10.09%	13.61%	16.16%

Data Source: MorningStar EnCorr, May 2011

Figure 71   The S&P 500 Index

Return by Holding Period	Minimum Return	Average Return	Maximum Return
1 Month	-21.54%	0.87%	16.81%
3 Month	-29.65%	2.67%	26.61%
6 Month	-41.82%	5.43%	41.84%
1 Year	-43.32%	11.00%	61.18%
3 Years	-16.09%	10.21%	33.30%
5 Years	-6.63%	10.69%	29.63%
7 Years	-3.85%	10.96%	23.01%
10 Years	-3.43%	11.34%	21.43%
15 Years	4.09%	11.88%	19.66%
20 Years	6.41%	11.85%	18.26%
25 Years	7.31%	11.76%	17.26%
30 Years	7.80%	11.29%	14.78%
40 Years	7.91%	10.90%	13.50%
50 Years	7.43%	11.04%	13.92%

Data Source: MorningStar EnCorr, May 2011

Figure 72 The MSCI EAFE Stock Index

Return by Holding Period	Minimum Return	Average Return	Maximum Return
1 Month	-20.17%	0.94%	17.87%
3 Month	-35.35%	2.91%	35.10%
6 Month	-44.84%	6.08%	54.09%
1 Year	-49.94%	12.73%	103.70%
3 Years	-19.30%	11.04%	58.36%
5 Years	-6.86%	11.14%	42.67%
7 Years	-2.32%	11.27%	32.41%
10 Years	-0.67%	11.24%	25.53%
15 Years	1.85%	11.91%	21.62%
20 Years	2.29%	11.62%	16.71%
25 Years	7.54%	11.91%	15.69%
30 Years	8.63%	11.25%	13.55%

Data Source: MorningStar EnCorr, May 2011

Figure 73 Barclay's Capital Intermediate Bond Baa Index

Return by Holding Period	Minimum Return	Average Return	Maximum Return
1 Month	-9.74%	0.72%	9.37%
3 Month	-12.68%	2.20%	18.09%
6 Month	-13.81%	4.46%	23.17%
1 Year	-12.68%	9.24%	35.18%
3 Years	-1.28%	9.10%	21.51%
5 Years	0.43%	9.08%	20.20%
7 Years	2.27%	9.21%	17.25%
10 Years	3.59%	9.52%	14.84%
15 Years	4.75%	9.54%	12.76%
20 Years	6.31%	9.56%	11.65%
25 Years	7.65%	9.53%	10.79%
30 Years	8.35%	9.36%	10.28%

Data Source: MorningStar EnCorr, May 2011

Figure 74   Dow Jones Credit Suisse Hedge Fund Index

Return by Holding Period	Minimum Return	Average Return	Maximum Return
1 Month	-7.55%	0.77%	8.53%
3 Month	-16.07%	2.40%	16.62%
6 Month	-19.49%	5.01%	23.66%
1 Year	-19.07%	10.40%	36.81%
3 Years	-0.44%	9.87%	25.17%
5 Years	3.52%	9.69%	20.00%
7 Years	5.51%	9.50%	14.54%
10 Years	6.00%	9.47%	12.94%

Data Source: MorningStar EnCorr, May 2011

Figure 75   MSCI Emerging Market Stock Index

Return by Holding Period	Minimum Return	Average Return	Maximum Return
1 Month	-28.91%	1.34%	18.98%
3 Month	-44.83%	4.25%	56.31%
6 Month	-55.75%	8.63%	71.13%
1 Year	-56.42%	17.42%	92.14%
3 Years	-18.18%	12.40%	46.66%
5 Years	-10.19%	11.96%	40.31%
7 Years	-9.28%	10.37%	29.11%
10 Years	-0.35%	8.06%	18.18%

Data Source: MorningStar EnCorr, May 2011

Figure 76 JPM EMBI Plus Emerging Market Bond Index

Return by Holding Period	Minimum Return	Average Return	Maximum Return
1 Month	-28.74%	0.93%	10.70%
3 Month	-30.32%	2.87%	23.76%
6 Month	-30.85%	6.09%	30.78%
1 Year	-29.87%	12.97%	48.23%
3 Years	-0.09%	11.91%	33.17%
5 Years	3.07%	11.61%	21.12%
7 Years	8.45%	11.91%	17.44%
10 Years	9.46%	11.91%	16.35%

Data Source: MorningStar EnCorr, May 2011
© 2011 Wells Fargo Bank, N.A. All rights reserved. Used with permission from Wells Fargo Bank, N. A.

Figure 77 Citi World Government Bond Index (WGBI)/Non-U.S. Developed Market Bond Index

Return by Holding Period	Minimum Return	Average Return	Maximum Return
1 Month	-7.53%	0.81%	9.30%
3 Month	-8.11%	2.49%	23.96%
6 Month	-12.55%	4.99%	31.10%
1 Year	-9.70%	9.94%	60.92%
3 Years	-4.11%	8.54%	34.93%
5 Years	0.11%	8.03%	19.11%
7 Years	1.01%	7.99%	18.28%
10 Years	4.39%	7.56%	16.50%

Data Source: MorningStar EnCorr, May 2011
© 2011 Wells Fargo Bank, N.A. All rights reserved. Used with permission from Wells Fargo Bank, N. A.

Appendix VIII

Summary of Retirement Vehicles

401(k): A retirement savings plan sponsored by for-profit companies that allows an employee to contribute pre-tax dollars to various investment choices. The U.S. Internal Revenue Service (IRS) sets the amount an employee can contribute to a 401(k) each year.

403(b): Unlike the 401(k), only employees of public schools and certain tax-exempt organizations can participate in a 403(b) plan. Like the 401(k), there are annual contribution limits to a 403(b).

IRA: An individual retirement account (IRA) is a personal retirement savings plan available to anyone who receives taxable compensation during the year. For IRA contribution purposes, compensation includes wages, salaries, fees, tips, bonuses, commissions, taxable alimony, and separate maintenance payments.

Keogh Plan: A qualified retirement plan that may be set up by self-employed persons, partnerships, and owners of unincorporated businesses as either a defined benefit or defined contribution plan. As defined contribution plans, they may be structured as a profit-sharing plan, a money purchase plan, or a combined profit-sharing/money purchase plan.

Roth IRA: Unlike a contribution to a traditional IRA, a Roth IRA contribution is never deductible. The Roth offers tax-*exempt* rather than simply tax-*deferred* savings. There are also income limits on Roth IRAs.

Traditional IRA: Whatever earnings you have on your contributions won't be taxed until you withdraw that money. There are income limits on traditional IRAs. If you earn more than a certain amount, you cannot invest "before tax" dollars, unless it is a 401(k) rollover.

Appendix IX

Components of International and Emerging Markets Indices

MSCI EAFE Index: An index that measures the performance of a basket, a stock market index of foreign stocks, from the perspective of a North American investor. The index targets coverage of 85 percent of the market capitalization of the equity market of all countries that are a part of the index.

Countries represented include the following: Australia, Austria, Belgium, Denmark, Finland, France, Germany, Greece, Hong Kong, Ireland, Italy, Japan, the Netherlands, New Zealand, Norway, Portugal, Singapore, Spain, Sweden, Switzerland, and the United Kingdom. The largest weightings include: Europe (excluding the United Kingdom), 46.5 percent; Japan, 21.2 percent; the United Kingdom, 23.1 percent; and Pacific (excluding Japan), 9.2 percent.

MSCI Emerging Markets Index: A free float-adjusted market capitalization index that is designed to measure equity market performance in the global emerging markets.

Countries represented include the following: Argentina, Brazil, Chile, China, Colombia, the Czech Republic, Egypt, Hungary, India, Indonesia, Israel, Jordan, Korea, Malaysia, Mexico, Morocco, Pakistan, Peru, Philippines, Poland, Russia, South Africa, Taiwan, Thailand, and Turkey.

Appendix X

Glossary of Investment Terminology

Accrued interest: Interest accumulated, but not yet paid. Most bonds pay interest either semi-annually or quarterly. Accrued interest is the interest that accumulates between interest payments.

After-tax return: The investment return after deducting the impact of taxes paid by the investor.

Alpha: The return provided by an investment manager over the respective benchmark return. Also referred to as "excess return," meaning return over the benchmark.

Annualized return: The percentage return over a year factoring in dividends or income, realized or unrealized appreciation, and factoring out withdrawals or additions.

Asset class: Types of investments that have similar characteristics. For example, stocks and bonds would both be considered asset classes.

Basis point: A standard measure of interest rate movements in the bond market (also referred to as BPS). A basis point is 1/100th of 1 percent. In other words, a 1 percent move in interest rates is equal to 100 basis points.

Beta: A measure of volatility. This can be used to measure a security against the market or a portfolio.

Correlation: A statistical measure of how different securities or asset classes move in relation to each other. For example, if asset classes have a high correlation with each other, they generally move in the same direction.

Dividend yield: The yield of a stock based on the dividends paid by the company. The calculation simply takes the annual dividends per share and divides by the price of one share of stock.

Earnings yield: The ratio of earnings per share to the current share price. It's the inverse of the price-to-earnings (P/E) ratio.

EBITDA: Earnings before interest, taxes, depreciation, and amortization. Some analysts and companies refer to this when discussing their financial results. There is considerable debate about whether using EBITDA or just plain "operating earnings" as the appropriate way to look at earnings. Personally, I opt for operating earnings because it deducts the interest, taxes, depreciation, and amortization, which, in my mind, are all real costs of running a business.

Efficient frontier: A line generally plotted on a graph with the vertical data being return and the horizontal data being risk (standard deviation). The line plots the "optimal" portfolio, which means that you would have the highest expected return for a given level of risk. Portfolios that plot below the line would be considered "inefficient" in that you are not theoretically maximizing the amount of return you could achieve for a level of risk.

Equity risk premium: The estimated excess return of the overall stock market over the risk-free return (typically, some short-term yield such as ninety-day Treasury bills).

Financial plan: A document that includes a full profile and risk assessment of the investor, a full balance sheet analysis, an outline of investor goals, the asset allocation framework required to meet those goals, and specific planning around topics, including taxes, education, retirement, debt reduction, etc. The format of the plan can vary greatly and is not as important as the content.

Large capitalization stocks: Stocks with market capitalizations generally higher than $10 billion. These stocks are often referred to as "large caps," or large companies.

Load fund: A mutual fund that has an upfront sales charge or commission generally used to compensate the salesperson.

Market capitalization: The value of a company calculated by taking the number of shares outstanding and multiplying by the current price of the stock.

Market cycle: The period between the two latest highs and lows of the market. It includes both a bull market phase (up market) and a bear market phase (down market). The length of a market cycle varies, but is typically at least five years.

Mid-capitalization stocks: Stocks with market capitalizations generally between $2 billion and $10 billion. These stocks are often referred to as "mid-caps," or medium-sized companies.

Modern portfolio theory: Developed by Harry Markowitz in 1952, this theory brought investment thinking from a world where risk and return were thought of in terms of individual stocks to one where risk and return are looked at from a portfolio perspective. The ideas of portfolio diversification and the mixing of assets that are non-correlated are important elements of this theory.

Monte Carlo analysis: A problem-solving technique used to estimate the probability of an outcome by running multiple iterations using different sets of data. This technique can be useful in figuring out your likelihood of meeting your goal with your existing portfolio.

No-load fund: A mutual fund that does not have an upfront sales charge or commission. This does not, however, mean that the fund is without any cost to the investor. Both load and no-load funds have internal management fees and expenses that are collectively referred to as the "expense ratio."

P/E ratio: A commonly used valuation measure for individual stocks or the stock market. The P stands for "price" and the E stands for "earnings." A lower ratio implies a market or stock that is a better value than a higher ratio.

Russell 1000: An index used to measure large company stocks. It is made up of the 1,000 largest stocks in the U.S. market. This index is often used to measure large-cap manager performance.

Russell 2000: An index used to measure small company stocks. It is made up of stocks ranked in size from 1001 to 3000. This index is often used to measure small-cap manager performance.

Standard deviation: A measure of the dispersion of returns around the mean, or average, return. The greater the spread, the higher the standard deviation, and the greater the volatility of that investment. Many investors use standard deviation as a measure of risk.

Sharpe ratio: A ratio developed by William F. Sharpe to measure risk-adjusted performance of a portfolio. The ratio is calculated by subtracting the risk-free rate of return from the rate of return of the portfolio, and then dividing that result by the standard deviation of the portfolio returns.

Small capitalization stocks: Stocks with market capitalizations generally between $300 million and $2 billion. These stocks are often referred to as "small caps," or small companies.

Tracking error: The standard deviation of the difference in the returns of an investment or a portfolio to the returns of the benchmark or index you are comparing against.

Tax equivalent yield: Pretax yield that is required of a bond for its yield to be equal to that of a tax-free bond. It is calculated by taking the tax-free yield and dividing it by one, minus the investor's tax rate.

Value at Risk (VaR): A calculation that takes the three components of time period, confidence level, and loss percentage or amount, and estimates the worst case scenario in a given time period. For example, VaR can answer the question of what your maximum loss would be at the 95 percent confidence level over the next one-year time period. This is a useful measure of risk in stress testing an investment portfolio.

Wash sale rule: An IRS tax rule that does not allow an investor to claim a tax loss on the sale of an investment that is repurchased within thirty days of the sale date.

About the Author

Dean Junkans is the Chief Investment Officer of Wells Fargo Wealth, Brokerage and Retirement, where he oversees more than $1.4 trillion in assets. He has held numerous leadership and portfolio management positions in his 28-year investment career. Mr. Junkans has personally managed high-net-worth and ultra-high-net-worth investment portfolios. In addition, he is active in speaking to clients and prospects about investing and the markets.

Media that have quoted Mr. Junkans include *Bloomberg News, CNBC, The Wall Street Journal, Money Magazine, Reuters, Associated Press*, and many other regional publications.

Mr. Junkans earned a Bachelor of Science degree from the University of Wisconsin at River Falls and a Master's degree from Purdue University. He is a Chartered Financial Analyst charter holder. Mr. Junkans is also a U.S. Army veteran.

Mr. Junkans has a passion for mentoring new investment professionals and has developed curriculum for university students interested in pursuing an investment career. In addition, Mr. Junkans serves on the Board of Governors for Bethel University Foundation. He is a member of Dean's Council of College of Business and Economics, University of Wisconsin at River Falls. He is also chair of the Advisory Committee for the new Investment Fundamentals Certificate being developed by the CFA Institute.

Mr. Junkans lives with his family in Minnesota.

CPSIA information can be obtained at www.ICGtesting.com
Printed in the USA
LVOW11s1255040814

397255LV00005B/184/P